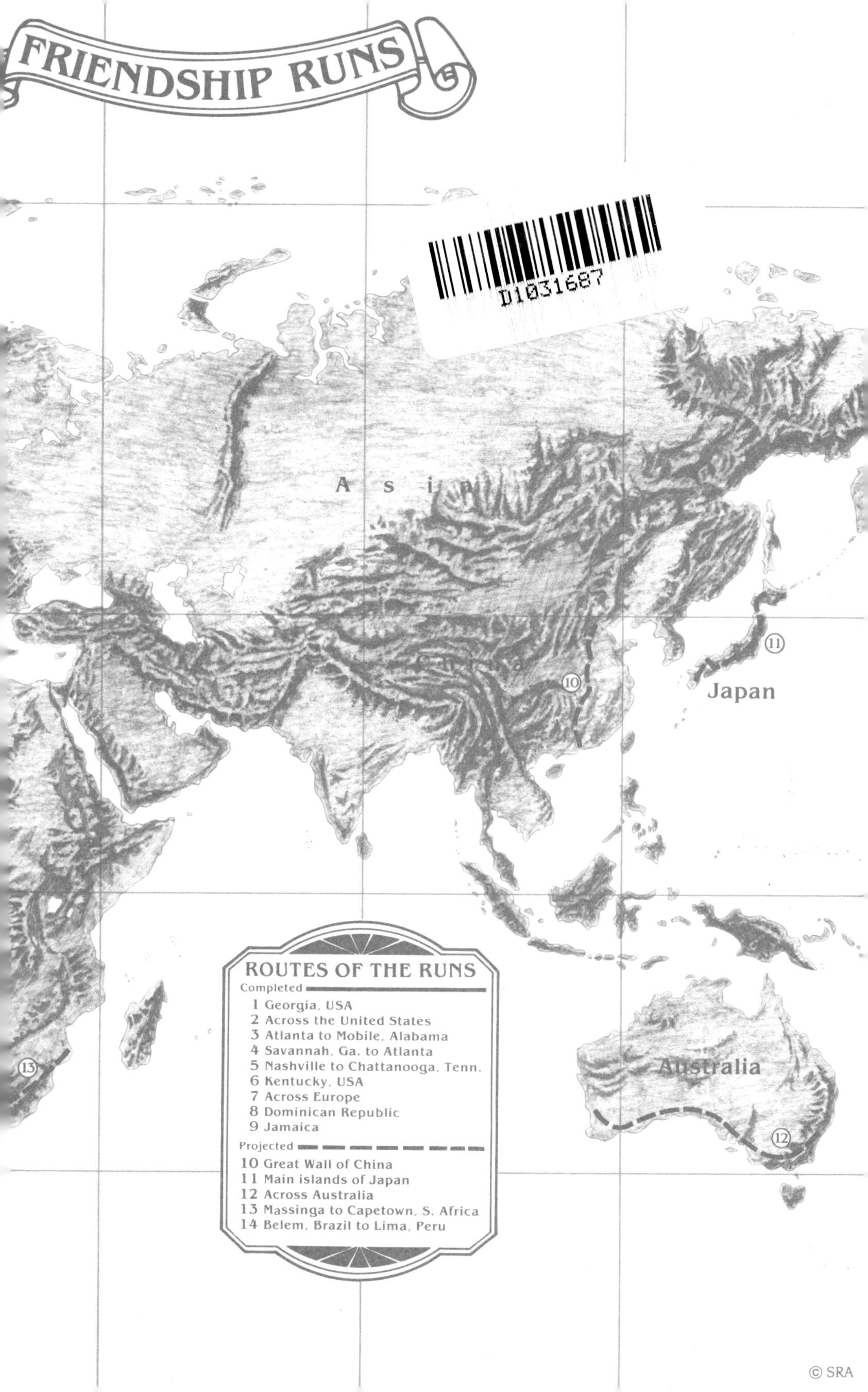
FRIENDSHIP RUNS
D1031687
Asia
China
Japan
Australia
10
11
12
13
ROUTES OF THE RUNS
Completed
1 Georgia, USA
2 Across the United States
3 Atlanta to Mobile, Alabama
4 Savannah, Ga. to Atlanta
5 Nashville to Chattanooga, Tenn.
6 Kentucky, USA
7 Across Europe
8 Dominican Republic
9 Jamaica
Projected
10 Great Wall of China
11 Main islands of Japan
12 Across Australia
13 Massinga to Capetown, S. Africa
14 Belem, Brazil to Lima, Peru
© SRA

11/23/97

No Mountain Too High

To
Laida Amarsi —
You're Pretty as a
Speckled Puppy Sitting
under a red wagon bed!
Your New Friend: Sam —
Sam Cottrell

STAN COTTRELL

No Mountain Too High

Introduction by
Ruth Bell Graham

Fleming H. Revell Company
Old Tappan, New Jersey

Scripture quotations in this volume are from the King James Version of the Bible.

Library of Congress Cataloging in Publication Data

Cottrell, Stan.
No mountain too high.

1. Cottrell, Stan. 2. Runners (Sports)—United States-Biography. 3. Sports—Religious aspects—Christianity.
I. Title.
GV1061.15.C66A36 1984 796.4′26 [B] 84-6775
ISBN 0-8007-1206-4

Printed in the United States of America

Dedicated to the memory of my father,
who taught me that there is no mountain too high—
my mother,
who believed I could climb every mountain—
Carol,
who has stayed beside me all the way—
my children, Michelle, Stan III, and Jennifer,
who provided a reason to never give up—
and to my many friends—you know who you are—
a special thanks for your encouragement during the climb.

Contents

Special Thanks

To Cecil B. ("Cec") Murphey,
who helped write this book,
who has learned to understand me and who,
most of all, has become my friend.

Introduction

You will find this not only an interesting book but a stimulating one, and inspirational as well. In fact, after reading about Stan's running adventures you might even find it exhausting. Anything but boring!

It has been my privilege to know Stan personally and he is worth knowing! I recommend the book wholeheartedly and am eagerly awaiting news of his forthcoming China run.

Ruth Bell Graham

Preface

"You're plumb crazy, Stanley junior."
"You'll never do it."
"You can't."

I've heard words like that all my life. Every time I dreamed big, I could always count on at least one person telling me I couldn't do it.

I heard it from Daddy often enough. Sometimes he called me an idiot. Teachers in school said or implied the same. My friends, with few exceptions, did little to encourage me. They didn't hold back their opinions either. Yet I rose above all those voices trying to pull me down. If I had listened, I'd still be in Kentucky, living on a farm, plowing a living out of those rocky hillsides.

For some people, that's a good life—there's nothing wrong with being a farmer in the hollows of Kentucky. But if I had listened to all those voices, I'd never have done much with my life; certainly I'd never have lived up to my potential. I have always wanted something more out of life. And I didn't give up until I made it.

For me, "making it" has meant setting records of physical achievement. In a word: running.

I ran from New York to San Francisco in forty-eight days, setting a record. I've had people tell me that they didn't believe it was humanly possible to run every day for forty-eight days and to cover a distance of 3,103.5 miles, *but I did believe.*

I also set a record of 167.25 miles for twenty-four hours of continuous running. In 1982, I ran across twelve countries of Europe, covering 3,500 miles in eighty days.

For nearly five years I've prepared myself to run the length of the Great Wall of China. Yet I've had one setback after another. Dozens of people have advised me to forget it. I won't forget it. And one day I'll run there. I know I'll do it.

Maybe that sounds like I am bragging. I don't mean it that way, but I've learned I can do just about anything I've decided to do. I've set goals and I've reached them, sometimes not right away, and more than once after failing. But I keep trying until I make it.

Yet sometimes it sounds strange for me to think of where I am now when I remember where I started. I had every reason in the world not to succeed.

Yet I am succeeding in spite of all the obstacles. Three reasons for this can be given. First, my mother taught me one valuable lesson. As far back as I can remember, she said to me, "You can do anything you want to do. With the good Lord's help, you can do anything." Those encouraging words of Momma's overrode all the negative voices.

Second, I don't know how to quit. Daddy especially helped me here. Despite his negative influences in my life, he taught me how to hold on in the midst of hardship. More than once I heard him say, "A Cottrell ain't a quitter." Those words became a part of me. At times, common sense tells me to stop, especially when the physical poundings tell me I can't go on. But something in me rebels every time I'm tempted to give up, or when anyone tells me I can't do it.

Third, I have one advantage that has made me an ultramarathon runner. Sports doctors who have examined me tell me that I'm a highly efficient human machine. To show you what they mean, I'll give you two examples.

Most joggers burn up approximately ninety to a hundred calories a mile. (As a rule of thumb, burning 3,500 calories equals the loss of one pound.) Can you imagine how many calories I would burn up each day, running fifty miles? I would have to consume *twice* the amount of food the average person requires to compensate for the lost calories plus my own daily needs.

However, my body converts food to energy so efficiently that I need only about one-third what most people require. I can run fifty miles, take in only 3,000 calories, and maintain my body weight.

I can also take the physical punishment of pounding the pavement for hours every day. I weigh less than 140 pounds. Experts estimate that at my rate of speed, every time my heel strikes the asphalt over 400 pounds of pressure jars my knees and legs. I've been running that way for a lot of years. I plan to keep on doing it.

I can't fully explain why I am who I am. I've mentioned a few factors. Certainly there are others. My father has been a dominant influence in my life and he still exerts a strong influence over me even though he is no longer living. For years I tried to prove to him that I could achieve almost anything. I believe that the desire to prove myself to Daddy instilled in me an unusual determination to win. I refuse to fail.

I've overcome the obstacles that branded me a born loser. That's partially why I'm writing this book. I want to help other people who may think they're losers in life. I want others to be able to say, "Stan Cottrell did it. I can do it too! I know I can do it!"

The height of conceit is for a person to say, "I can't." Anyone who thinks that way—given his natural ability plus all the opportunities in the world—is communicating a message of determined defeatism. Those words really say, "I won't win no matter what you say or what you show me."

And most of us get what we aim at!

In one sense I've always known I was a winner. I may not have had the big dreams, but through Momma's constant message—"Son, you can do anything"—and Daddy's dogged determination to stick to anything he tried, I grew up knowing I could win. I've always struggled at the same time with what people call self-esteem or the self-image.

A part of me balked at winning in life. It was like a voice inside me said, "Who are you to think you can bust out of here?" Maybe that determination to keep fighting is what made me able to see that I was a winner. Winning meant, not having great talent, but not giving up.

When I start getting low or when failure stares at me, I remember something that happened to me in 1982, near the end of my run across Europe. I had been running fifty miles every day. In southern Spain I raced across rough terrain on the seventy-sixth day of my run. As I mentally calculated it, I knew I was right on schedule. Despite my exhausted body that cried out for relief, I knew I could complete the run in the projected eighty days.

Just then, I started up a steep mountain. As though the land had a personality, I screamed at it, "You're not too high for me. I'm going to beat you because no mountain's too high!"

I thought of my past successes. I envisioned those of the future. No high mountain of any kind would ever defeat me. Then I saw a road sign ahead of me. I don't know Spanish, but I had enough sense to realize that *sierra nevada* meant one thing: mountains. And not simply mountains, because I had been running through them for days—but high mountains, very high ones.

I rethought my words. *No mountain too high.* High mountains or low valleys wouldn't make any difference. I picked up my pace. I could do it. Those mountains almost won, but my hold-on attitude kept me going when I didn't think I could possibly take another step.

I've faced a lot of other mountains in life. And I still do. But I know none of them are too high. By sharing my experiences with you my hope is that you'll also believe there's no mountain too high. It has become the theme of my life. I hope it will become yours.

A friend of mine, country and western singer and recording artist Rose (Rose Mac) McFarland, has written a song to express the theme of my life. It goes like this:

> Let me tell you there's no mountain too high
> for you to climb.
> Just look up and say, "I'll capture it—
> with God's help, and a little time."
> Even if it looks as though it reaches
> to the sky,

Take it step by step. You'll find it's not really
  all that high.
Once you start down the other side,
You'll look ahead, and smile with pride,
'Cause God gave us no mountain too high.

I believe that! Succeeding doesn't come easily. It never does. You'll make mistakes and you'll experience setbacks. But keep on. Shut out negative voices. Cry out, "No mountain too high!" when you encounter your next obstacle. From your inner being, shout to the world, "I can do it!" And you will.

Stan Cottrell's Running Records*

1955	Won his first race at age 12—100-yard dash at a county fair.
1956	Won a 2-mile cross-country, age 13.
1960	Won four first-place awards at a Hart County track meet, age 17.
1961	On a dare, ran from Horse Cave to Munfordville, Ky., 10 miles; won $5 and had name in the paper for first time.
Aug. 13, 1963	"Tennessee on Foot or Bust"—attempted to run across Kentucky, age 20.
Apr. 19, 1964	Placed 92nd in a field of 342 as the first Kentuckian to enter the Boston Marathon.
Oct. 31–Nov. 6, 1978	Ran across Georgia, 405 miles.
Sept. 24, 25, 1979	Set record for distance run in 24 hours (167¼ mi.) at Lovett School, Atlanta, Georgia.
Oct. 22, 1979	Second attempt to run across Kentucky (completed 82 miles).
May 16–July 3, 1980	Set the record for running across America, New York to San Francisco, 3,103.5 miles in 48 days, 1 hour, 48 min.
Oct. 24, 25, 1981	Ran across Kentucky, 146 miles in 33 hours.
Feb. 3–8, 1982	Carnival for Cure Run, Savannah to Atlanta, 276 miles.
Sept. 20–Dec. 7, 1982	The Great European Adventure Run from Edinburgh, Scotland, to the Rock of Gibraltar, 3,500 miles in 80 days.
May 18–20, 1983	The Dominican Republic Tropical Paradise Friendship Run, 146 miles. Repeated in March 1984.
Oct.–Nov., 1984	The Great Friendship Run in China (projected).

* A selected listing.

No Mountain Too High

1
A World Record in Forty-eight Days!

When you've dreamed of something for ten years and then it finally happens, it's hard to believe it's real. That's the way it was for me on my "Run for America." Even after I left New York City, I still couldn't quite believe that it had all come about.

Forty-eight days later, on the morning of July 3, 1980, I wasn't thinking about the realization of a dream. I was thinking about my feet. They felt like two wads of hamburger. Each step brought a new thrust of pain from my groin to my toes. Despite the pain, I knew I could make it. After all, it was a short run that day—only twenty miles.

Twenty miles to a nonrunner sounds like feet pounding a lot of pavement. But I had already completed over 3,000 miles in forty-seven days. This was my last lap on the run from New York City to San Francisco.

I tried not to think of the mileage. That's always a defeatist way to run because you keep thinking, *only sixteen miles . . . only fourteen more. . . .* Your whole concentration goes into ticking off each quarter mile and that wastes energy.

Instead of miles and my own pain, I thought of what had happened in the realization of this dream. Most of all, it was amazing to me that I, a kid from the hollows of Kentucky, would be vying for the world's long-distance record.

Only the night before, twenty-one-year-old Tommy, one of four people who followed me in the van all the way across the States, had said, "Stan, do you realize that your life will never really be the same after tomorrow?"

"I'll be the same Stan, no matter what happens," I replied.

I didn't know what to expect when I reached the end of the run. I had hopes and a lot of ambition. But I was positive that no matter what changes took place in my own world, I'd still be the same Stan. I didn't understand then, or until a long time later, that when events change in our lives, we change too.

That last day, forty-eight days after leaving New York, I didn't dwell on things like that. I had dreams of the world rushing to congratulate me, and of having my name in the *Guinness Book of World Records.* Maybe I can be forgiven for thinking about worldly acclaim because on that day it all seemed certainly to be happening. That morning a San Francisco radio talk-show host joined me for the run, and went alongside me for fourteen miles, broadcasting a little of our conversation from time to time so that the whole Bay Area was kept abreast of my progress.

He fitted me with earphones like the ones he was wearing and, after we got started, he asked me: "What's it feel like, Stan, to be running today?"

"Like I'm near the end," I said. It was all I could think of at that point. I was so near attaining my goal I would have preferred to have said: "Just stick with me for a few more miles and then we can really talk." I didn't think he would run with me for long, but he was obviously in shape. He did "stick with" me all the way to the Golden Gate Bridge.

I was running through the lovely seaside town of Sausalito when the road made a turn. Then for the first time in my life, I saw the Golden Gate Bridge stretching across the bay. I tried to emboss the picture on my mind so that later I could recall its impact on me.

When I reached the bridge itself, the area swarmed with TV cameras, reporters, photographers, helicopters, and even a motorcycle escort. For a moment I ignored the crowd, wanting to glimpse that magnificent bridge up close. It was even more impressive than from a distance.

Suddenly everything was happening at the same time. People yelled at me from everywhere. At times the helicopters dipped low and the noise deafened me.

At least two hundred people lined the bridge, cheering me on. I heard, "Almost there!" "Keep going, Stan!" But with all the noise and excitement it was only a sea of faces. In those minutes it was as though a videotape played before my eyes. As I tried to focus on those cheering faces, in my mind I saw other faces—faces of those who had encouraged me to make this cross-country run. I also saw the faces of those who told me I was crazy and would never make it.

In the midst of the exultation a helicopter zoomed down so close I could hear the pilot talking to the station about my run. Noises came from every side of me and blended into a kind of indistinguishable roar. Mesmerized by everything going on around me, I had momentarily forgotten my physical torture. Suddenly people blocked my path; everyone shouted at the same time. Someone thrust a bottle of champagne into my hands. "Drink it!" a voice yelled out.

I'd never had a drink of champagne in my life and I wasn't about to start then.

"I don't drink," I said, slightly embarrassed because of the hovering of reporters and broadcast people.

"Do something with it!" a voice barked.

"The only good thing for that stuff is to pour it out!" I said.

"Pour it over your feet," someone said.

"Just do something with it," hissed the man who had given it to me.

For a moment I felt sorry for him. He had obviously planned it so that I could publicize his brand of champagne. Hardly conscious of what I was doing, I sat down, pulled off my shoes and socks, and poured the cooling liquid over my burning feet.

"Hold it!" a loud voice said. I looked up to see a man position himself to get another picture before I finished the entire bottle. People all around me snapped pictures. The wire services picked up this photo and sent it all over the country. Fortunately, they didn't identify the brand; the man didn't quite get the kind of publicity he had wanted.

Hurriedly I put on my shoes and socks again. My feet were so swollen and tender I had to ease the cotton over my now nailless toes.

The run resumed. I was following the schedule set for me by the news media. The last two days of the run, for me at least, had ceased being an athletic feat and had become a media event. I understood what they were doing and I wanted the publicity, even though I felt slightly self-conscious around all these people.

An entourage of spectators, police escorts, and TV people followed me right to City Hall where I had planned to finish. The media people had asked me to complete my run just before 11 A.M. in order to get the best coverage. I arrived at City Hall at 10:48, having covered the official distance of 3,103.5 miles.

Friends from my boyhood hometown of Munfordville, Kentucky, had flown to San Francisco to see me complete the run. They tried as a group to get to me, but couldn't penetrate the police barricade. My mother and my wife waved to me. At the moment, that was the best contact we could make.

As I neared the finish line and could see the banner stretched above the street, I had a strange feeling in the pit of my stomach. It struck me that as I moved forward I was in the present and moving toward a goal, but two feet over the finish line would make it a past event—something over and completed. My dream accomplished. I wondered what I'd feel like.

Just as I ran under the banner, a military band struck up "The Star-Spangled Banner." School children cheered me. Several politicians, standing in front of City Hall, welcomed me to San Francisco. Then the press interviews began.

So much happened so quickly in the next few hours, I could scarcely keep it all straight in my mind. A lot of speeches followed the remarks by a representative of the mayor's office. One was by an army general.

Suddenly for me it was all over. I had done it—I had completed my "Run for America." Aside from the tiredness of my body, which I had no time to think about, I felt caught up in this strange event going on around me. People kept pumping my hand and asking questions. So many begged me to pose for pictures that I wondered if I could ever relax my face and stop smiling.

While one part of me told me that the excitement had to end, I refused to think about that now. I had completed the run of 3,103.5 miles. I, Stan Cottrell, the little fellow from Kentucky whose father used to think would never amount to much, had broken the world's record. Someone might come along and beat my time, but no one had done it before me. (Later, someone did run in a shorter time, but he ran from the West Coast to the East, which is easier because of the wind. Going west from Kansas I fought headwinds most of the way. Going east, those same winds become tailwinds, propelling you forward.) I wanted to enjoy that day and savor how great it was to see my dream come true.

For two days I went from interview to talk show to TV program. I was on "Good Morning, America" and, it seemed, almost every local station in the Bay Area. The hype and the excitement were every bit as great as I had expected.

Two days after completing the run, my wife Carol and I had reservations to fly back to our home in Atlanta. When we reached the airport for our flight home, a swarm of people waited for us. More pictures, interviews, and good wishes followed. Best of all, we had a few minutes to talk with our old friends from Kentucky who had brought my mother and had come to see me finish the run.

Upon our arrival at Atlanta's Hartsfield Airport, local TV, radio, and newspaper reporters flocked around my family and me. This made me feel especially proud. It was such a warm feeling to come home to a hero's welcome.

As we walked off the concourse, I realized that young Tommy had spoken with true insight. I wouldn't be the same again—I couldn't be. I had tasted success and public recognition. I could never be content to go back to obscurity again.

I had returned with a high sense of anticipation. I was now a celebrity. Someone in Hollywood would appear at any time, eager to buy the film rights to my life story. Dozens of corporations would vie for the opportunity of having me advertise their products the way Bruce Jenner and Cathy Rigby had done following their triumphs. I knew that from this point on, life would rush into full gear and everything was going to be great!

It didn't take long for realism to set in.

The first bombshell hit at the Atlanta airport. Among the cheering well-wishers, process servers awaited me with warrants for my arrest. They had no intention of arresting me, but they served the warrants anyway. I owed money—a lot of money.

Expenses for my Run for America had soared beyond my calculations. We had underestimated everything, especially the costs for my crew. A doctor flew in twice to check my condition; we also had an advance person for public relations, a photographer, and two drivers for the van that stayed behind me all the way. During those six and a half weeks we had provided for our own food and clothing as well as travel expenses. While keeping track of the mounting costs, I didn't worry too much. After all, once I had completed the run, offers would pour in and I'd wipe out my debts.

I remember thinking how hard it had been to make that run. During the previous eighteen months I had earned exactly two hundred dollars. We lived on Carol's earnings as a schoolteacher—$8,600. Not only had we not earned much; we had used up every bit of our savings on expenses prior to the run. We even mortgaged our house.

But my big break would come any day, I thought. I had such confidence that I went around in a euphoric trance, absolutely assured I was on the brink of cashing in. Mentally I had already made plans about things I wanted to change around the house and the new car I'd buy.

When the process servers met me, I didn't feel disturbed. "Good to meet you," I said, and shook their hands. "You'll have the money soon." I had no doubts about that. After all, I had just broken the world's record for long distance running in forty-eight days, one hour and forty-eight minutes. I was famous. The offers would pour in.

They came all right. Then the nightmare began.

2
Deals, Dreams, and Disaster

I loved it when the telephone rang. A single tinkle from that object made my adrenaline pump. After sixty calls—even a hundred—each one had the same effect. This would be *the* call. I was positive.

Not just the telephone, but the mail. Letters piled up with offers for me to use a particular product and endorse it. One company wanted to sell Stan Cottrell T-shirts. Writers contacted me with grandiose ideas of ghostwriting my story and making both of us a fortune. I didn't know much about writing, and I learned pretty quickly that most of them didn't either.

Ironically, the first day I was home I answered the doorbell for the fortieth time and a deputy sheriff from DeKalb County stood in the doorway. He took off his hat, and with an embarrassed smile said, "I'm sorry, Mr. Cottrell, to have to do this to you." And he handed me still another warrant.

"It's all right," I assured him. I laughed and made some silly comment that right then I had enough of them to paper one bathroom wall. "But," I hastily added, "I'll have it all worked out soon."

"Oh, and—and would you mind giving me your autograph for my son?" he asked as he thrust a paper and pen at me.

I laughingly obliged.

"I'm sorry to have to do this, Mr. Cottrell," he said again. "Honest."

"I understand," I said and slapped him on the shoulder. "Just doing your duty." I pointed to the dining room table. "See that pile of papers? Offers of all kinds. I'll soon have all this money problem straightened out."

"Sure hope so, Mr. Cottrell," he said, and apologized a third time.

With fortune just around the corner I wasn't going to worry about another warrant demanding immediate payment. In a few days—weeks at the most—I would satisfy all my creditors.

Offers kept coming. The only trouble was that none of them worked out. Either I didn't believe in the products themselves or the people who pushed them didn't strike me as on the level. But I didn't worry. The right promotion or the right product would come.

The first week after my return to Atlanta, I didn't want to leave the house. Every time the phone rang I knew it just had to be a TV or movie producer calling to buy my story, or someone who had the right deal for me.

I had made that run for a lot of reasons. First, of course, was to challenge the limits. No one had done it before and I knew I could. And I suspect that many of us like the challenge of doing something no one else has done before.

Money and my future had a lot to do with the run across America, too. I expected to use the publicity to launch a new career for myself. By being recognized as the world's greatest long-distance runner, I hoped to catapult into product boosting. I envisioned only a bright future for myself.

I know that, in addition to all this, I ran because of the need for self-affirmation. For most of my life until recently I have needed to prove myself, largely because I never seemed to come up to my father's expectations of me in my younger years. Although I had finally gained his approval, I still needed to prove to myself that I could succeed in anything I set out to do.

For a full month I stayed close to the house, never leaving for more than an hour, and always making sure someone was present to answer the phone. The second month crept by, and then the third. Day after day, men in three-piece suits carrying black attaché cases rang my doorbell. Each had a golden deal for me. I grew tired of hearing the word *deal.* I wanted an opportunity. Finally, four months of phone calls and personal visits had come and gone and the phone stopped ringing. The celebrity status in my own neighborhood had ceased. I was just plain Stan Cottrell again, a peculiar fellow who runs long distances. Depression began to set in. I couldn't understand what was happening.

After the run I had called one of the executives at Keds, the shoe company that cosponsored the run. "Are you going to do anything with me or not?" I asked impatiently.

"What did you have in mind?" he replied, genuine surprise in his voice. "You might come to see me and we can talk about it."

Keds had helped sponsor my "Run for America" and I had been sure that at least they would call me and cash in on the publicity. They had even developed a new shoe for runners. This shoe, reasonably priced, promised additional comfort and yet weighed less than most running shoes. (They never marketed the shoe.) Unfortunately for me, Stride Rite had acquired the parent company. The new management, caught up with their own internal problems, kept their interest in me at a minimum.

Only when I talked to the executive did I realize the truth. My thoughts had been aimed toward the future and I had assumed an ongoing relationship with them, even though they had never made any promises to me. It dawned on me that the reason for their sponsorship was not an interest in Stan Cottrell; they saw it as a great way to test their new shoes. My running proved that they held up and were as good as they had expected.

At the Keds main office in Boston the executive listened patiently when I went to see him. He must have been touched by my predicament or else felt that they had a moral obligation to me. Keds came to my rescue.

For the next 118 days I traveled almost constantly around the United States on behalf of Keds. They produced posters showing me running across the flatlands of Kansas, wearing their shoes. I had trekked 2,094 miles on the first pair of Keds—which showed it was a superior shoe. (I figured that 600 or 700 miles before signs of serious wear is about normal.) I finished the Run for America wearing the second pair and continued wearing them later. I'm sure I got at least the same number of miles from that pair as well.

During the four months of traveling, I held seminars, was interviewed, and even talked to prospective buyers. It was a heady time and I was beginning to dream of great things happening to me in the future. I saw myself as Keds' living symbol.

Then, in February 1981, the same executive who had sent me on the road, called. He treated me kindly but he said, in effect, "Our company has decided not to promote the running shoe. That being the case, we won't be needing your services anymore."

That came as a shock to me, but I was still flushed with excitement. It took a few days for the impact of that decision to crumble my world.

For the next four months I drifted from day to day. I did my daily runs of twenty miles without enthusiasm. I spent time with my family, but my voice was edgy—even I knew it. But I didn't seem to know what to do about it. I easily diagnosed myself as being depressed, but I had no idea how to snap myself out of it.

During that four months, I still received offers. A movie company flew me to California and talked about how wonderful a film would be on my life—but I never heard from them again.

A writer persuaded me to let him write my story, and he even showed me an outline. He had contact with a New York publisher and assured me that they would snap at the chance of publishing my biography. Then came the publisher's letter of polite rejection.

Other deals that had seemed so great fell apart for no apparent reason. I would get excited about a project. The representative would leave me with words such as: "Man, this is absolutely the greatest. You'll be hearing from us very, very soon." I seldom heard anything more.

Each time a new promoter came my way, I felt like the dumb sheep following its leader to the slaughter. Each great deal fizzled.

I not only became depressed about myself, but about people in general. Aren't there any real people anymore? Is everyone a hype salesman? I couldn't get answers to my own questions. After a while I didn't even care.

I grew tired of seeing little men carrying their little briefcases, wearing profuse smiles, wanting to sign me up. Even their words blurred so that every deal-maker sounded like the one before him and the one who followed.

Why are they wasting my time? I asked myself a hundred times. *Is that the way they go through life, trying to make deals and yet doing nothing? Making promises they can't possibly fulfill? Do they constantly prey upon people like me?*

Along with a movie contract and book outline, my files contain forty-two other deals, options, and promotional strategies offered to me. For instance, a beer company offered me a million dollars.

"I'm not a beer drinker and I couldn't peddle anything I don't believe in," I told the representative from the company.

Part of my answer came from principles taught me from childhood. Momma and Daddy both always told us, "Stand up for what you believe in, and speak up when you don't agree."

Probably the real reason I turned down all that money had to do with Daddy himself. For the first eighteen years of my life, he drank heavily, sometimes got mean, and often beat me. I always vowed I'd never get like that, so I left liquor alone.

Even though I turned down that million-dollar contract, I still didn't worry. Another deal would come along—an even better one. I remained optimistic.

While waiting for the right project, radio stations called and interviewed me. A couple of sports magazines featured me. I appeared on national TV shows—Dinah Shore's "Dinah and Friends," and "P.M. Magazine." With that exposure, I knew someone would call with the opportunity I was waiting for. Surely they would say, "I saw you on television and I'd like you to. . . . " But they didn't. I walked around in a haze of confusion and shock. Things weren't going as I had planned. I hadn't counted on all those negative aftereffects.

After four months I felt I had but one choice. I would go back into the business world. Previously I had done well professionally. I had been the top salesman for a pharmaceutical company. So I tried getting a job. My TV appearances looked great on a resumé. But they also hurt me.

One personnel officer said, "Stan, I'd like to hire you. Your resumé looks good. But you wouldn't stay. You'd only work for us until you'd built up enough of a nestegg to start running again."

"That's not so," I protested. "I've had my fling. I'm through with that." I genuinely meant it, too. I leaned forward on the desk, trying to mask my desperation. "I've done what I set out to do. I've proved to myself that I can do it."

He shook his head slowly. "Sorry, Stan, we just can't take a chance."

I didn't plead with him. Maybe he knew me better than I knew myself. I had to admit to myself that I probably would have set up another run if I had the financial backing.

I had a lot of dreams still in my heart. But with the doors closing around me, I had decided that's all they were—dreams. I had been so sure that after breaking the world's record and getting all the publicity, fame and fortune would fall into place and I could have all the things I'd dreamed of. I had gotten close to success. I had traveled far from the cow pastures and barnyards of Kentucky. But I couldn't even earn a living.

3
Daddy

With all the excitement and hype surrounding the Run for America, I had one regret. Daddy hadn't lived to see it. He had died in January 1980.

"He would have been proud of you," Momma said.

"I hope he would," I said. But then, I had always hoped Daddy would be proud of me. In one sense, I've spent most of my life trying to please him and make him proud of me. People have often told me he was, but I never seemed to hear it. For example my younger sister Pam wrote me in 1983, after she and I had enjoyed a good visit:

> I wanted Daddy to be as proud of me as he was of you. You were always the one he bragged about and listened to and referred to as "my son says. . . . " I know you probably don't know all that, but it seems like that's all I heard for so many years.

I hadn't known "all that." I was always trying to live up to my father's expectations—expectations that I assumed he set for me. I had an inner compulsion to try to please him.

Daddy was hard on me and strict. From early childhood I knew what it was to work from before sunrise till dark. Hard work became a habit with me and I owe that to Daddy and Momma.

Because I was the oldest of six children, Daddy naturally put more responsibility on me and expected more of me. In the part of Kentucky where we lived, the code of the hills played a large role in our lives. By this unwritten code, we learned to put qualities such as honor and responsibility to the family above all else.

According to the code, fathers made rules and children obeyed. Whatever my daddy did was right simply because he was Daddy.

Momma also treated us strictly, but with a wide showering of affection. She never contradicted Daddy, but she did hug us or say something kind when Daddy tore our hides up from a good whipping.

Most of my growing-up years we lived in a kind of shack. Daddy prospered and made living conditions nicer later in his life, but that happened long after I left home.

My childhood memories go back to that shack. I used to watch Momma carry water from the pond to heat for cooking and bathing. Although people often laugh about Saturday night baths, that's exactly the way it was in our house. In warm weather, Momma took us children to the pond, making us boys turn our backs while the girls got their baths.

I didn't think of it as impoverished because I had nothing to compare it with. Only after I started school and met other children who had nicer houses, with such luxuries as running water, did I begin to feel ashamed of my own home.

Daddy, for instance, raised hunting dogs. More than anything else he loved fox hunting. He always kept ten, sometimes as many as fifteen hounds tied up in front of the house.

As I got older, I learned that other people didn't have dogs filling up their front yards. They actually had grass and trimmed lawns. I became ashamed when anyone visited us, not only about the yard full of dogs, but all that went with them—the unbearable odor, their manure everywhere so you had to step carefully, but mostly their constant howling. When people visited, it would take minutes just to quiet down the hounds so that we could talk to each other. But Daddy loved his dogs and they were very important. He was the kind of man who didn't care much about what other people thought anyway. He did what pleased him.

Daddy stood six three, 230 pounds of solid frame; he was physically tough. He expected me to grow up to be the same way. But I never did get big like my father. I took after my mother's people. At my full height, I still stood more than half a foot shorter than Daddy.

As I was growing up, Daddy kept waiting for me to get big like himself. When he saw no spurt of height, he convinced himself that I had worms. If his dogs didn't get big, he gave them worm pills and once they were de-wormed, they started putting on weight.

"You're wormy, boy," he'd say, and I came to learn what that meant. So did my sister Shirley, and the others. We'd scream and try to run away. But it didn't do any good. One way or another, we took the worm pills. But no matter how many de-wormings, I never exceeded five eight-and-a-half.

I grew up believing that I disappointed Daddy in every way. Even though it doesn't make much sense, somehow I felt that it was my fault for not getting taller. Daddy had been athletic and had done well in high school sports, especially basketball. He had always wanted a son to play basketball and he said it often enough. To please him, I tried—really tried—to play sports in school. But I was too short for basketball and too small for football. There was only one thing I could do well—run. But in those days, people didn't have much respect for running.

"If you weren't so wormy, you could play basketball," Daddy would say to me, as though I could will myself taller.

I don't know how many times he'd put his hand on my head and apologize to his friends for my lack of size. Usually he did that after he had been drinking a lot.

And Daddy could drink! The first eighteen years of my life, I saw him drunk regularly. When he drank, he got mean. And when Daddy got mean, he sometimes beat us all, but especially me. More than once, when Daddy beat me he'd say, "I'm doing this to loosen up your hide to make you grow!"

I didn't understand my Daddy. He didn't talk much, especially about his feelings. We lived a hard life. Daddy worked hard and drank hard. He also worked us hard. When I was six, he took me to the barn, put me on a stool, and set me under a black Angus heifer.

"Here's how you milk," he said and showed me. From that day on, as long as I lived at home I milked the cows.

Somebody once chided him for working his children so hard. "What you raising those kids for?" the man asked. "I'm raising them for my own use," he said and walked away.

Sometimes I'd get discouraged and wondered if life would always be like this—hard work that never seemed to end. Yet I had some happy times as a child. We played in the barn. And we swam in the local swimming hole. Even though it was cold until near the end of summer, by early June we boys would dive in naked.

The really bright part of my growing up, however, was Momma. From the earliest days of my life, she'd hug me and say, "You're going to be a special person someday." Somehow she knew I could achieve. She never let me forget that I could do anything I wanted to do in life.

I needed her because Daddy gave me the opposite message. Not only did he make remarks about my size, but he often humiliated all of us, not caring what anyone else thought. For instance, once he bought a pair of hand clippers for hair cuts. So that he wouldn't have to cut our hair often, he'd grab me and my younger brother Harold and shave us bald. When we got to school, the other children laughed at us.

Daddy used to buy our blue work shirts at auctions. I had four shirts at a time and they usually lasted me about three years. When we didn't have shirts, he'd take us to the feed store and let us pick our feedsacks so that Momma could make shirts for us boys. He always bought pretty prints for the girls' dresses. He'd take us to the hardware store and buy us boots, the kind that came up above our ankles with both buckles and laces.

My father drank regularly and did crazy things. Once, angry with a town constable, he drove into town in his pickup, carrying two shotguns. He stopped in the middle of the main street, fired several times in the air and yelled, "I'm looking for the constable." The man wisely never showed himself.

Another time we came to a farm where he wanted to talk to the man. The front gate had a lock on it, so Daddy pulled out his gun, shot the lock off and drove on into the farm. When his friend came out of the house, Daddy smiled and said, "Sorta messed up your gate."

I think everyone was afraid of Daddy. No one ever talked back or argued with him. He lived with violence all the time when he was drinking and would fight over the simplest remarks.

I hated being around him when he was drinking because I never knew what he was going to do. One time, my feet were as sore as they could be with what we called dew poisoning. It happened because we kids went barefoot from the time school let out in late May until it started again in September. Running across the fields, we would stub our toes and get cuts on the soles of our feet. Moisture from the grass would seep into these open cuts, causing infection. Sometimes the swelling went up into our ankles. On that occasion, I had dew poisoning and Daddy said he wanted to see me dance.

"My feet hurt so bad," I answered.

"Dance, boy!"

"I can't!" I cried, trying to hold back the tears.

"At least jump up and down."

I did. I jumped up and down, just as he told me. And because I was hurting so badly I cried out, "Oh gosh dern! Oh gosh dern!"

To my father, that was not innocent language. It was cursing. And it made him so mad that he took a switch after me and whipped me so badly that I couldn't lie down on my back for a week. "I'll teach you to cuss," he said.

When he'd really get angry he had a favorite expression for me. "You damned idiot!" he would say. But when he said idiot, it came out like "ee-dee-ott."

"I'm not an idiot, Daddy," I said more than once. "Please don't call me that."

"You're still just a damned idiot!"

By the time I was eight or nine I did the work of a man, and he made sure I did, too. Yet no matter how hard I tried, he never said anything encouraging. But he always noticed when I didn't do something right.

Sometimes Daddy would be drunk and come into the house and

start kicking things around. One night he kicked over the table and yelled, "I've killed before and I'll kill again." (He referred to an incident long before I was born, when he had killed a man in self-defense.) In his drunken mood he scared us.

Momma grabbed us and we all ran from the house. We spent that night hiding in the woods. And that wasn't the only one. We spent many nights in gullies and ditches, hiding from him until he sobered up enough for us to return home.

Another person who influenced me as a youth was my great uncle, Roy, Daddy's uncle, who came to live with us when I was five. Uncle Roy had held a responsible position with a railroad company in Louisville, was married and the father of three children. But his drinking absolutely ruined him.

When Uncle Roy had nowhere else to go, he came to live with us. Daddy put a cot in the smokehouse and fixed it up a bit, and that was his home. He became a farm hand and one of my best friends. He was a buffer between Daddy and me and I learned a lot about life from him, though some of it was distorted by Uncle Roy's outlook on life.

Uncle Roy would drink like you wouldn't believe. We have an expression that describes his kind of drunkenness—"knee walkin', commode-huggin' drunk." That's how drunk he would get. I was with them on numerous occasions, because he would take me with them to beer joints. Uncle Roy and Daddy taught me to drink.

Once, Daddy stood me up on a soft drink case in a honky-tonk, gave me a roll of nickels and warned everyone, "My son is playing the slot machine and nobody's going to say a word."

Uncle Roy and Daddy regularly got into brawls with the other tavern patrons. And more than once, I joined in.

One of the craziest things to happen—and this time Momma really put her foot down—took place one Saturday afternoon. As he always did, Uncle Roy bought bootleg whiskey from the moonshiners. That day he kept handing me a bottle. "Here, hun," he would say. "You want a little drink? You want another little drink? Ol' Uncle Roy will always take care of his boy." I liked the taste because they had some way of using burned sugar that made it "tongue-slappin' good." By nightfall I was drunk out of my mind.

When Daddy started to drive us home, I was in the back of the pickup. Just as the truck moved, I jumped out and fell into a pile of coal, skinning my face and arms badly. Realizing that I was drunk, Daddy took me down to the pond to sober me up. But Momma came down and saw me floating face down in the pond, in pain from all the abrasions I had gotten from my fall. She threatened to call the sheriff to come and get Daddy.

When I was 15, I had my last drink. Uncle Roy and Daddy and a toothless friend had taken me with them on a three-day fox hunting trip, bringing along eight gallons of moonshine. One night, Uncle Roy and Daddy drank so much that they passed out. The next morning I awoke with the first rays of sunlight. There were Daddy and Uncle Roy, their faces unshaven, lips discolored from dry moonshine and saliva, flies swarming around them. I was so disgusted at what I saw that I vowed then never to drink again.

Uncle Roy lived with us until he became ill and had to go to the hospital. He had loved me, but his wasted life haunted me. My biggest fear was that some day I would make something of myself and then lose it all like Uncle Roy had done.

I've written a lot of negative things about my father, but it's also important to say that I never hated him. In a strange kind of way, I loved him. And in his own way, I think he loved me as much as Daddy could love anybody. But when you're a child, you can't reason all of that out. I could only feel that no matter how hard I tried, it wasn't good enough. I blamed myself for not having his approval. Either I had done something wrong or not enough of the right.

When I was young and saw everything in black and white, good or bad, I asked Momma, "Why do you stay married to him? He's so mean and drinks so bad."

Momma stared at me as though I had asked a question she had never thought about before. "Honey," she said as she wrapped her arms around me, "I married your daddy for better or for worse. I'm going to stick by what I promised."

"But he treats you so bad—"

"Hush, Stanley junior, I can't have you talking about your daddy that way." In all those years I never heard her criticize him or allow us to either.

My parents never fought, at least not that I ever knew about. Daddy said what he thought and no one challenged or argued.

While I never saw any demonstration of affection between them, it was there. We all grew up knowing that our parents loved and respected each other.

Momma is a religious woman. She always prayed and read her Bible and tried to teach us to live right. All through my growing up years those teachings stayed with me. We learned the code of the hills, mainly from Daddy's emphasizing it, and Momma taught us her religious convictions.

We honored our parents by quiet obedience. We learned not to criticize or question their decisions, and almost never did they ever get any backtalk from us.

The code said parents trained their children right. And being trained right meant doing it Daddy's way.

Momma always prayed a lot. Several times she told me that she prayed for every one of us children every single day. She also prayed every day for Daddy. Twenty years after she married him, God answered one special prayer.

On New Year's Day 1961, Daddy came into the living room and looked at all of us for a minute. Then he walked over to the big family Bible that Momma read from. Laying his hand on that Bible he said, "I'm never going to take another drink as long as I live."

Until the day Daddy died, eighteen years later, he never took another drop of liquor. I don't know what changed him or what brought it about. He never told anyone. He was secretive like that and no one ever knew what was going on inside his head. One thing about Daddy we all knew: when he made a promise he kept his word.

"I prayed for twenty long years for him to quit his drinking,"

Momma said. "The good Lord was a long time in answering. I kı
God would be faithful in answering my prayers. And He finally di

I don't want to give the impression that life was always miserable for me. Daddy quit drinking and I never saw any more of his meanness toward us, but we never grew close. In fact, Daddy had no idea of how to get close to anybody.

The one release I had was my running. Not that I thought of it as therapy, but it was. Running was the one thing I did well and enjoyed. Hardly a day passed when I didn't run, often for long distances.

I can still vividly remember one day when I was seven. I saw a jackrabbit in a nearby field. Suddenly I wanted that rabbit for a pet and took off running after him. It was early in the morning, perhaps eight o'clock. I chased that rabbit as he dodged, hopped, and backtracked. I got tired, but I was determined I wouldn't stop running no matter if it took all day.

Somewhere around high noon that poor rabbit just fell over and gave up. I picked up the furry creature and carried him home.

"Look, Momma, I got me a rabbit for a pet!" I said in excitement.

Momma smiled and shook her head. "Can't raise an animal like that in captivity."

"Sure I can!" I answered. After chasing that rabbit all morning, nothing would stop me from having him as a pet. I think, looking back, that I also wanted something that would be mine—just mine.

Momma laughed, and, convinced of my seriousness, finally said, "Guess you'll have to find out for yourself."

I played with the rabbit all afternoon and then made him a simple little pen to stay in for the night. The next morning I ran outside as soon as it was light, to play with my rabbit. At first I couldn't find him and wondered if he had escaped during the night. Then I saw what had happened. Our cat had attacked the rabbit during the night and killed him. I stared at the remains of that creature, not wanting to believe what I saw.

For the first time I had tried to have something that belonged only to me and I couldn't have it.

I threw the furry remains down and took off running, wanting to get as far from the house as I could. Tears streaked my cheeks. I cried for that little rabbit, but mostly I cried for myself. "I can't ever have anything of my own!" I screamed those words again and again.

Later, when I returned home, I felt a lot better. As I got older, I realized how much running helped me cope with pain and stress. Even at seven years of age, running had become one of the most important things in my life.

After I started school, I had to milk the cows every morning. Sometimes it took so long that I would have to run to catch the school bus, a mile from our house. Usually I ended up running all the way to the bus. Many mornings I'd miss the bus and that meant I had to run another six miles to school. I don't think I minded very much, especially in good weather.

I didn't like school much, because others laughed at me. We were the poorest children around. Our shack of a house was more than a mile from the schoolbus stop. On rainy days, Uncle Roy would put me and Shirley and Mary on the back of a mule and walk us down the muddy path to the bus stop on the gravel road.

I had so little training I hardly knew how to act in school. I can still remember the time in first grade when the teacher beat me for swearing. I didn't know I was swearing because I was only repeating words Daddy and other men used around me.

She grabbed me and gave me a good switching. And it hurt. My embarrassment probably hurt as much as the physical pain. Then she stopped and held me by the shoulders.

"Stanley junior, are you ever going to cuss again?"

"Oh, hell, no," I sobbed, "if you just won't whip me anymore."

She dropped her arms and looked strange. I could hear voices giggling in the background. "Sit down," she said. I never did find out if she quit because she thought I was incorrigible or finally realized I didn't know any better.

My school work ranged slightly above average and I didn't try especially hard. I showed no outstanding traits, even with running, until I entered sixth grade.

That spring the family went to the County Fair. I learned that they were having some running events, open to anyone, and I asked Daddy if I could enter the 100-yard dash.

"Aw, don't bother with that stuff," he said.

"Please, Daddy," I asked, "let me."

"Running's nothing, Stanley junior," he insisted.

"But please, Daddy!"

He shrugged his shoulders and walked away. That was the closest he usually came to giving outright permission, so I hurried over and entered the run.

I wore heavy boots and jeans already too tight and too short. All the other racers were bigger than I, most of them from high school. It didn't occur to me that I wouldn't win. Even though I felt strange next to all of them, as soon as the whistle blew, I took off. And I won first place.

People kept coming up to me and saying things like, "You're no bigger than a bar of soap after a good washin', but you sure can run."

"Don't see how you did it," others said.

"You're the fastest little kid I ever saw."

"If you're this good now, what'll you do when you get to high school?"

It was one of the proudest moments of my life. I felt as though I was as tall as any high schooler when the judge pulled me in front of everyone and pinned a ribbon on my faded blue shirt.

Back home I was the hero for several days. Everyone wanted to see my ribbon. I wore it to school every day for the next two weeks.

A small event, perhaps, but winning that race changed the whole course of my life. At last I found something in which I could excel and it was something I loved. No longer was being small a liability.

4
Too Small for Basketball, Just Right to Run

We lived for a time in Tennessee and folks in our area became accustomed to seeing me running. As often as they saw me, they still were amazed by it. "Why you running so much, Stanley junior?" I must have heard that question a hundred times.

"Cuz I like to run," I answered. I didn't understand *why*. In fact, I thought their question sounded silly. I liked to run; that was enough of a reason for me.

The worst part about people seeing me run was that they teased me, and some of the teasing was cruel. Like calling me "Knothead." Knothead Berry, who lived in the neighboring area, had been kicked in the head by a mule when he was a boy. It left him badly retarded and with a knot on his head the size of a grapefruit. Often he spent hours chasing a mule down the road, only to catch him, and then let him go. Other times he walked for eight or ten hours and couldn't remember where he was going.

"I'm not Knothead," I cried out, especially when Daddy called me that name. My protesting only seemed to make it worse.

The thing I remember most about living in Tennessee was that I saw my first cross-country meet, not just a 100-yard dash like I had won. It fascinated me. These were people like me. Many of them were my size, and they loved to run. For the first time, I realized I wasn't peculiar because I loved to run.

When I heard about the cross-country run, I signed up for it. The name, cross-country, was a joke to me, because I thought it would be twenty or thirty miles. It was only two miles. I signed up anyway. It gave me a chance to get with other boys who understood my zeal for running.

I was thirteen, in the seventh grade, and most of the boys were older. As we started to run, I breezed along, enjoying myself. I noticed how hard everyone was puffing.

"Why you breathing so hard?" I asked a couple of them.

"You getting tired already?" I called out to others.

I won the race easily. Everyone cheered me and I kept wondering why they made such a fuss. It was only *two* miles.

The following year, I ran in my first real track meet. I went there wearing my hightop tennis shoes but the city boys and those who had been coached wore track shoes with spikes. That was the first time I had ever seen track shoes. When I went home, I was determined to have a pair myself. I got four nails, and decided to nail them into the bottom of my shoes. Dad came out into the smokehouse and saw me.

"What in the name of sense do you think you're doing?"

"Making track shoes," I said.

"Making what?"

I explained about the track meet and the way the others had dressed. By now I felt ridiculous, realizing I couldn't make those nails stay in. Daddy shook his head, mumbled something about his idiot son, and left.

The following year we moved back to Kentucky, to a farm called Gobbler's Knob, four miles outside of Munfordville. This was to be my home from the tenth through twelfth grades. In Tennessee in ninth grade I had been on the track team and had done quite well. But the Kentucky school didn't have a track team. I wanted to run so badly that during my senior year I transferred to a school thirty-five miles away. I often had to hitchhike or beg a ride so I could get there, but it meant that much to me to be able to run.

During the tenth and eleventh grades, I had my first love. Her name was Elizabeth and she was dark haired, five feet four inches, and weighed about a hundred pounds. She lived across the river, and I would run over there to see her when I could.

Daddy made us go to bed at 8:30. Many nights, once I knew he was asleep, I'd sneak out of the house, and run over to Elizabeth's to talk to her. More than once I stayed until midnight. Then I'd run back home. Daddy used to wonder why I looked so tired in the morning, but, so far as I know, he never found out about these night visits.

Elizabeth always encouraged me. "I believe in you," she'd say. "I know you're going to be somebody important in life."

I could hardly believe she liked me. Beth was so pretty, and she had her pick of other boys around, but she liked me. Next to my mother, she was the second person in my life who encouraged me. "I'm proud of you, Stanley," she said more than once. I'll always be grateful for that encouragement.

At the time we met, a song called "Running Bear" hit the pop music charts. The kids started calling me "Running Bear" and Beth "White Dove," after the two lovers in the song.

When they called me Running Bear, I always felt it was a respectful teasing. They were complimenting me in a way teens compliment one another.

Of course, not everybody meant the teasing as respect. A few made vicious, cutting remarks. There was a man in town, recently released from a mental hospital, who walked about for miles each day. "Is he kinfolk of yours?" a few asked. "He must be your brother because he walks and you run!"

Beth buffered these remarks. "Don't listen to them," she said. "They're just jealous."

When I was in the eleventh grade, Hart County sponsored a county-wide field meet. All three of the county schools participated. It was the first track meet held in our county and I entered the 100-yard dash, the 220 and 440, ran on the relay team, and threw the discus. I tried eight events in all. Of the eight, I won four first-place ribbons, three seconds, and a third place for the discus. I was proud of those ribbons, yet I didn't feel comfortable wearing them. Beth kept raving over them, so I gave them all to her. She wore them on her dress all day. She was not only proud of me; she wanted everyone else to be proud, too.

A few days later I had a free period at school, so I went over to the Home Ec. room where I knew I'd find Beth. No one else was there.

We talked for a few minutes and I kept thinking how wonderful she was and how pretty. I glanced around quickly and, seeing no one else in sight, I leaned over and pecked her on the cheek.

Just then I heard a scream and turned around. A teacher, Mrs. Hensley, stood not five feet away. "You! You immoral boy! What are you doing?"

I hung my head, too embarrassed to answer. I finally mumbled, something like, "Well, uh, I—I."

"I saw what you did!" She kept repeating those words. The more she screamed, the worse I felt.

"I'll teach you to kiss one of our girls!" she said; then she grabbed me by the collar and dragged me all the way down the hallway to the principal's office.

Although I was as tall as she was, her grip on my collar brought mortal terror to me. "Please . . . I won't do it again . . . honest. . . . " My words only seemed to make her walk faster.

She jerked me into the principal's office and without giving me a chance to say anything, told him what I had done, not once, but several times. Her voice never calmed down to a normal level.

I felt terrible, as though I had committed adultery in public. No punishment would be too severe for me, or so I felt at the moment. The principal dismissed Mrs. Hensley, lectured me on my poor manners, and poorer judgment, ending with "Save that stuff until you're away from the school." He kept me in detention for a week.

Instead of discouraging me, this only inflamed my youthful love more. Beth had always stood by me. When she heard about my punishment, she said, "Then don't do it again on school property."

"Can I do it somewhere else?" I asked.

She only smiled.

How could I ever forget Beth? Always there when I needed her during those high school years. She stood by me no matter how strange people thought I was.

Daddy didn't like her, however, and more than once when her name came up, he'd say, "Why do you want to see that girl?" Daddy didn't want me to get serious with Beth, and marry her, because he didn't care at all for Beth's father. His dislike for that man is the sort of stuff of which feuds are made.

Daddy himself had gone to college three years just before World War II. Then he served in the army. After the army he didn't want to go back to college so he started farming again.

He was restless in those years and tried a lot of things. He failed in most of them due to his drinking. I have one vivid memory of his trying to drill for oil. He borrowed money and drilled wells on land within a fifty mile radius of our home. Thirty empty holes. He never did hit oil.

What I remember most is not the empty holes, but Daddy's response. He would decide there was no oil and would go home, discouraged. I'd think, *He's given up.* Yet, the next morning he'd be right back out on the land, drilling in a new spot.

"You can't keep a man down who keeps moving," Daddy said to me almost every time he started new drilling. To watch him go about it, anyone would think that every hole was the first one. He drilled with such enthusiasm and he'd say, "I know I'm going to strike oil here." He always believed that. His persistence taught me that just because a man fails once, doesn't mean he fails forever. He kept on trying and he taught me to keep on trying too.

Life wasn't easy for my father after coming home from the war. He had a family to raise and had to earn a living. Sometimes I wonder if that's why he drank so much. He had been out in the broader world, had a good education for his day, but it never seemed to do him any good. Perhaps in his frustration he turned to drinking and fighting.

During my senior year, a new coach came to Munfordville. His name was Ray Summers. I met him the day he arrived and I showed him around town and introduced him: "Meet our new basketball coach."

My Daddy had always wanted me to play basketball and I figured that if I became a good friend of the coach he would let me play. I wanted so badly to be on that team. I believed that if I could play, somehow I could compensate for my lack of height and that I'd become an invaluable player. Of course, that would also mean that I'd please Daddy.

I practiced hard and long. But one day I got the bad news. Mr. Summers said to me, "Stanley, this is one of the hardest things I've ever had to do. I'm cutting you from the team."

"Cutting me? You can't."

"No one trains harder . . . you try more than anyone else. . . . " He stumbled with his words, trying to be kind. But I didn't hear the kindness. It hurt too much.

"But I tried so hard," I said.

"Stanley, I know—"

"I'll even sit out the whole season on the bench. Just—just let me be part of the team. *Please.*"

"Don't make it harder on me, Stanley," he said.

"But I can play—I play better than a lot of those guys—"

"No one's more dedicated . . . no one works harder . . . " he said.

He never explained why he cut me. He didn't have to, because I knew, and I knew all along that it was coming. I just didn't want to face it. I tried hard to make the team, perhaps too hard. No one moved faster than I did. I would grab the ball and dribble across the court better than anyone else. But I had two weaknesses. I slammed into other players every time I raced across the floor, not intentionally; I just never seemed able to stop in time to avoid a collision. I had that ball and I moved toward the basket.

Even more, I was not a team player. I'm more of a self-competitive person. I play against myself, always trying to do things faster or better. My speed compensated for my lack of height, but it didn't compensate for my lack of team spirit. I tried too hard and ended up doing everything wrong.

When Coach Summers told me he had cut me, I stared at him.

Despite myself, the tears flowed and I couldn't hold them back. More than the pain of being cut from the team, I felt as if my whole life had crumbled before me. I wanted to show Daddy that I could succeed at something. I wanted him to see that I could play basketball. Then he'd be proud of me. Now I would never have the chance to show Daddy anything.

Hardly knowing what I was doing, I grabbed a baseball bat and, as I stared at the coach, anger filled my brain. He stood nearly a foot taller, but I screamed, "If you so much as bat your eyelashes wrong, I'll knock the living hell out of you!"

I think he understood, because he stood there, watching me and saying nothing. After a long silence between us, I threw the bat to the ground and walked away.

My reaction to being cut from the team reveals something about me that I was unwilling to face then. I had a mean temper and tended to settle things in only one way, by fighting. I didn't know how to control my temper and could get out of line very easily. I had learned to fight from Daddy and Uncle Roy and this mean temper would get me in trouble more than once in my young years.

At this time I was only one month into my senior year of high school so I transferred to E-town (Elizabethtown) High School, thirty miles away. I chose that school because it had both a cross-country and track team. I tried out, made the team and ran in competition until Christmas vacation.

On New Year's Day, 1961, in that part of Kentucky we had the largest snowfall on record: twenty-eight inches. Daddy said it would take weeks before all that snow melted. He knew what he was talking about. Schools closed for twenty-eight school days. However, the E-town High School was one of two schools in the state that stayed open. But I had no way to get there. To miss all those days meant that I couldn't possibly graduate in the spring.

This brought me to a real dilemma. Because of what I had said to Coach Summers, I couldn't go back to Munfordville. And I couldn't get to E-town. So I transferred to Cub Run High School, sixteen miles away, as soon as the schools reopened in February. Unfortunately, they had no track team. But I kept running anyway.

During that year I learned that colleges award scholarships. Because of the reputation I had established as an athlete in both Munfordville and E-town, I applied for a scholarship from Western Kentucky State College, forty-three miles away at Bowling Green. Western Kentucky had just started a cross-country team. The scholarship, worth sixty dollars, was a partial one; it would pay my tuition and books for a semester. It was probationary because I would have to prove that I could make the grade academically.

If that scholarship came through I saw it as my one-way ticket out of Munfordville and my first step toward success in life. I wanted to succeed at something. *Anything.* I hadn't defined any clear-cut goals, but I wanted to prove I was somebody. Too short for basketball, but just right for track—maybe there was a chance for me. With scholarship aid, I could make a life for myself—away from home and everything I had grown ashamed of.

I liked those days at Cub Run. I worked at part-time jobs in the drug store and the grocery store—the nearest thing we had to a supermarket—earning forty to fifty cents an hour. That spring I also tried out for the junior-senior play and won the lead. At the end of the play, I received a cup as the best actor of the play. Things were looking up.

5
"A College Degree Ain't Worth Much"

Following high school graduation, while waiting for college to start, I worked at several part-time jobs. I didn't have much money or much time. But I did manage to go out with Beth on Friday and Saturday nights.

The big thing to do, as far as teenagers were concerned, was to go to the local drive-ins, and then hang out at the root beer stand. I don't remember any of us going out on single dates; it was always a group affair.

One summer night after a movie, my friends and I went to the root beer stand in Horse Cave. All kinds of kids were there, laughing and having a good time.

"Hey, Running Bear," Tommy Joe Turner called out, "Still running?"

"Sure am," I said. "Every day."

"You think you can run a long ways, don't you?" someone else said. They were all doing this in fun and I joined in with it.

"Can you run ten miles?" Billy Howard asked.

"No problem," I answered, because I knew I could.

"Bet you five dollars you can't," answered Steve Scott.

"Yeah, and I'll bet you another five dollars," someone said.

I knew I could run that far, but there must have been some doubt because I started to think of all the money I'd lose if I tried to cover a bet from everyone. They finally agreed that it would be a single five dollar bet for me to run the ten miles from Horse Cave to Munfordville. They had one rule: I couldn't walk—not even a single step. If I walked, I lost the bet.

It was 10:30 P.M. when I started to run. For the first two miles, my friends followed in their cars, swerved around me, honked, and yelled. After a while they began to worry that maybe I'd make it after all.

Twice cars roared ahead and pulled off the road. Then the guys jumped out to scare me. I kept running. One of my friends called the sheriff's office in Munfordville and reported me: "There's some crazy maniac who escaped from a mental institution and he's running down the road toward Munfordville. You better stop him."

Carl Hughes, the town policeman, pulled his car alongside me and turned on the spotlight. "Stanley junior! Have you lost your mind? What you doing out here?"

"Sorry, can't stop to talk, Carl," I said. "I got a bet with these doggone fellas and I can't stop running. If I stop I lose."

He laughed, realizing why he had been phoned, and said, "Keep on going, Running Bear!"

Someone timed me. I ran the entire ten miles from the root beer stand in Horse Cave to the Tastee-Freeze in Munfordville—ten whole miles—in sixty-two minutes. I wore only tennis shoes and cut-offs, but I ran for all I was worth.

As I ran I remember screaming out at them in my thoughts: *I am somebody! You can make fun of me, but I'll show you! I am somebody!*

I crossed over the Green River bridge and didn't stop until I came to the town limit. By this time, carloads of kids had gathered around. For a trophy they handed me a torn sheet, with the words "Horse Cave to Munfordville" written in magic marker. They tied the prize money up in a corner of the sheet—five dollars in pennies and nickels. I felt so great and enjoyed it so much that I invited everyone to the Tastee-Freeze for Coca-Colas. I spent all my hard-earned prize money on everyone else.

We laughed and joked together. Twenty years later many of these friends would greet and encourage me as I tried for higher goals.

Jo Snider, a Munfordville reporter, wrote an article for the town paper. "Darers Have to Pay Off," it said. It was the first article written about me:

> A group of our young men-about-town thought they had made a good wager when they bet Stanley Cottrell, Jr., $5.00 that he couldn't run from Horse Cave to Munfordville. . . .
>
> He is some runner, and a college which has a good track team will do well to look him over.

For the first time I began to believe in myself because of the constant support from Momma, the frequent encouragement of Beth, the visible achievement through my running, and especially my winning the cup for acting. When Daddy called me an idiot it no longer bothered me. At last I realized I wasn't an idiot!

Two weeks before graduation I went in to see the principal, Mr. McRedd. I had taken no college prep courses, but it had become absolutely essential to me to go to college.

I'll always remember that scene in his office. He leaned back in his chair as he listened to me. He chewed tobacco and kept a Folger's coffee can by his desk. From time to time, he'd pick up the can, spit into it, and chew some more.

"What are the chances of me going to college?" I blurted out. I hurriedly told him that I had applied for a partial scholarship for the cross-country team at Western Kentucky University (called Western Kentucky State College at that time) which would pay my tuition and books.

Mr. McRedd heard me out, spit tobacco juice again, and shook his head. "Well, I'll tell you, Stanley junior. First, you ain't got no sense. College is for smart kids. You got to be real smart to get into college and stay there."

"I think I can do it," I said.

"You don't want to go away to college and get your mind all filled with big ideas. Then you have to come back and live on a farm again."

"I want to go to college," I persisted, not sure if my nervousness showed or not. After all, this was the principal speaking to me.

"Join the army if you want to do something. Then come back and marry that little kinky-haired girl I saw you fooling around with over in Munfordville. Still going with that little girl?"

"Yes, I am," I said.

"Pretty thing. Marry her and forget college."

"I want to go to college!"

He kept on talking, speaking nicely, trying to convince me that a kid from a poor home with only average grades didn't have any sense dreaming about college.

As he talked, I felt the weight of all the rejections in my life. I thought about Daddy's calling me idiot and always criticizing. I remembered my being cut from the basketball team. I thought of a hundred other times when I had been hurt. But this time, instead of making me back down, it only made me mad.

"Mr. McRedd, I'm going to show you! I'm going to college and I'm going to make it!"

"Maybe so," he said and spit into the can again.

I walked out of his office, my fists clenched and my mind made up. More determined than ever before, I vowed that I'd not only go to college but that I'd graduate.

I didn't realize it then, but I was already learning to climb mountains when people said I couldn't. And that's one of the most valuable lessons I have learned about life: *just because people say you can't do something doesn't make it so.*

When Western Kentucky awarded me a scholarship to run cross-country, I was happier than a new rooster in a hen house. From then on, I knew nothing would stop me from going to college.

On the day I left, Daddy came up to me and handed me $6.50. "That's all I got, son," he said, and walked away.

He didn't need to explain. In those days, $6.50 was a lot of money for Daddy to give me. I hadn't expected anything. Daddy was losing his best field hand, but he still wanted to give me some kind of help. Six dollars and fifty cents was his way of saying, "I'm for you."

I had only one pair of "Sunday-go-to-meetin' " britches, and the crotch was ripped out of them. They were dark blue. Momma didn't have any black or blue thread to match so she sewed them up the crotch with red thread. She cried to see me go off to school like that, but there was nothing she could do.

Years later, when I got my first good job, I told her at Christmas that I would get her anything she wanted—a refrigerator, a sewing machine, anything. She thought a moment and said she would like a few spools of some pretty thread. I went to the store and bought her a hundred dollars' worth of thread in all the pretty colors they had!

I hitchhiked to Bowling Green and enrolled at Western Kentucky. I earned my rent and food by helping take care of the house where I lived with nineteen other boys. I didn't have much, especially compared to most of the others. But then, I'd never had much before, so I didn't really mind.

I ran with the track team and made every practice. I also did a lot of running on my own. Two miles was considered a good, long run then. I often went ten.

People didn't know as much about running in those days as they do now. I got all kinds of crazy advice. "You're going to get your heart pumping so hard it will explode!" one coach told me. For days afterwards, I made sure I didn't exceed ten miles. I kept fearing that any step I took over ten miles I'd develop an "athlete's heart" or worse, that I'd blow up. Of course I never suffered any bad effects, but for a long while I half expected to.

Some of the others ran faster than I, but I never seemed to tire out. I could participate in every event and still have energy left. Running with the team and on my own became my major release from pressure. Floating along the roads, oblivious of everything else, I was free, really free. Marking mile after mile gave me the assurance that I could make it at Western Kentucky and anywhere else in life.

Working took a lot of my hours, but I was used to that from my high school days. When grade reports came out, I had pulled down 4 A's and 3 C's. During that first term I studied hard—the hardest ever in my life. I had determined to make it in college and nothing would stop me. That first grade report convinced me that I could make it.

While in college, I joined the Marine officer training program and a year later the Marine Corps Reserves. Daddy let me know that he didn't like it. He hated the marines. After his own stint in service, he said he never wanted his sons to go in. "Marines are the first ones to fight and the first ones to get killed. I didn't raise my son to be cannon fodder."

That first summer, fifteen hundred of us signed up and many dropped out. In our platoon only eleven of the original fifty made it, but I stayed in and went to all the required drills and programs.

College had many bad moments for me. One time I got into a fight. A big, tall, drunken student began yelling at me about marines, calling them jar-heads. He was egging me on to a fight. I tried to get away, but he chased me. My daddy had told me, "Son, never look for trouble, but be ready when it comes." This drunk student caught me, started pounding my chest, and knocked me against a soft drink machine. Somehow I picked up an empty Coke bottle and smashed it against his face until he passed out.

Winning that fight by beating a guy nearly twice my size earned me a lot of respect. "No one messes with Cottrell," became the slogan. Two of my fellow marine candidates bragged to the officer in charge about what I had done and concluded, "The Marines came out on top." But it cost me. A few days later I received a letter from the Marine Corps. It contained my discharge for "improper decorum and conduct unbecoming an officer."

I went out for a long run. I had learned by then that running was my best therapy. Sometimes, when I didn't know how to handle a situation or when life became too hectic, I would go for a run, and when I came back, I always knew I could cope.

"This is the end of my life," I kept saying. "I had a chance to make something of myself and I blew it. I'm a loser—like my daddy says."

Even though I wasn't religious, I also remember asking, "God, why are You doing this to me?"

I received my discharge just as the fighting was building up in Viet Nam. Later that year, five of my college friends went to Viet Nam. All of them died in battle.

I stayed in college. In my junior year, I had another fight, this time over a girl. The dean of students didn't expel me but suggested I drop out of college for at least a semester, and I agreed. Actually, I had something else in mind anyway. About that time, a man who had run in the Boston Marathon visited our campus and talked to some of us about it.

A marathon measures 26.2 miles. The Boston Marathon, one of the oldest, is also one of the roughest, most grueling runs. They hold it on April 19, which is still winter in that part of the country. The man who told about his experience didn't even complete the race. He had dropped out after nineteen miles.

"He ran nineteen miles without stopping," one wide-eyed girl said.

"Nineteen whole miles," another said.

I listened, thinking, "I could easily do nineteen."

But I had no time to dwell on a marathon run because I had to go home to Munfordville. By then, Daddy had made some changes. He owned a gas station and was even making a little money at it, though the financial pressure on him was heavy.

The station, filthy from the lack of anyone to clean it, embarrassed me. Daddy hired me to work for him and I usually ended up working sixty to eighty hours a week. This gave me a lot of free time between customers so I spent the time cleaning and scouring the place.

The worst part was that most of the country men chewed tobacco. They would just spit on the floor and nobody seemed to pay any attention. I got the place cleaned up and waited for Daddy to tell me how nice it looked. But he didn't say a word. The next thing I knew, Daddy spit on the floor—a long line of juice from his chewing tobacco.

"Dad!" I blurted out. "I've worked hard to clean this place up and scour away all that tobacco juice and look what you did!"

He glared at me for a long second, and then said, "Son, this is a country gas station and I deal with country folks. If you want to work in a nice city where everything's clean and nice you just go there!"

Before I knew it he said, "You just get out of here! Just get out of this station and don't come back!" I never argued with him and I knew he meant it. So I left.

With free time and no job I realized I could compete in the Boston Marathon. So, on April 12 I hitchhiked to Boston. I had never been out of the South in my life and had no idea of the temperature in New England in April. I left Kentucky wearing a pair of cut-off jeans and a sleeveless college sweatshirt. In a bag along with my running gear I carried a couple of shirts, an extra pair of jeans and my toothbrush. I had twenty-five dollars in my pocket.

As I traveled northeast, the rain turned to sleet, and then to snow. Once along the way a man who gave me a ride put me out of his car in a driving rain, for no reason, and I became thoroughly soaked. A New York state trooper came along shortly after that and took mercy on me, driving me to a truck stop twelve miles away in Erie. There a waitress fed me donuts and coffee and got me a ride to Boston with a trucker. I was already coming down with the flu by then, and helping the driver unload his shipment of produce in Buffalo nearly did me in. I arrived in Boston five days after leaving Bowling Green, sick and feverish—and a little wiser.

From another runner I learned about a free clinic and went there to get enough medicine to keep me going. After waiting more than an hour, I finally saw the doctor. He took my temperature and whistled. "You need to get to bed, son."

"I can't," I said, afraid he would say something like that. "I've come all this way from Kentucky just to run the Boston Marathon. I've got to run."

"You've got to go to bed!" he said.

A kind man, he sat down beside me and asked me a few questions about why I wanted to run. A nurse gave me an injection. Then he gave me samples of penicillin so that I wouldn't have to pay for a prescription.

"I advise you to get right into bed. Stay there for at least a week.

With a temperature of 104° you need to sleep and rest." He smiled, "But, with your kind of determination, I doubt that you'll follow my advice."

I remember shaking my head and saying, "I'm going to run. Even if it kills me, I'm going to run."

I went to the YMCA where I stayed for two dollars a night for four days. Most of the time I stayed in bed, sleeping a lot, determined to be well enough for the big day. I didn't have a chance to cover the route of the marathon. All my concentration went toward getting well.

On the day of the race the outside temperature was barely above freezing and it was raining lightly. My temperature registered 102°. Sick or not, nothing was going to stop me from running. I decided that I might die during or after the race, but I was going to complete the 26.2-mile course.

Each step, from the very first mile, brought spasms of pain. My lungs burned and my head ached. But I kept going. When I reached "Heartbreak Hill," six miles from the finish line, I could see the Boston skyline. I wanted badly to give in then and stop. But something within wouldn't let me.

"I've got to hang on," I kept saying to myself. "I've got to hang on."

Somehow I made it to the end. I placed No. 92 in a field of 342, which was the biggest turnout in the Boston Marathon history. I was the first Kentuckian to run the marathon.

I didn't think about my position in finishing or my time. In fact, I didn't think about anything. As soon as I passed the finish line I collapsed. When I became conscious, two people stood over me and another knelt beside me. "You all right?" a strange voice asked.

"Yeah, fine," I said and made them let me get up.

I was too sick to eat the traditional serving of beef stew at the end of the race. Later I went back to the cheap hotel where I stayed. I lay down and slept straight through for fifteen hours. I remained in Boston for two more days, getting medication from the free clinic. A doctor there who was also from Kentucky treated me especially well. Then I hitchiked back home.

News about my running in the Boston Marathon made the local papers. Strange. I had been running all my life. I had been the best runner on my high school team. I had been a member of a college track team. All of that didn't seem to mean anything. But running in a national event like the Boston Marathon made it different in the minds of the people around Munfordville. At least they now took me seriously. No one ever called me Knothead again.

But, Boston Marathon or not, I had to do something with myself. So I went back to work for Daddy, helping him manage the station and sell used cars. This time I didn't worry about cleaning the floors! I worked sixty hours a week, often eighty, at the rate of fifty cents an hour. Even then it was slave wages, but he was my daddy.

I stayed through the whole year, and realized as never before that I didn't want to stay in Kentucky. I had seen enough of that larger world out there and was determined to get into it. So, I reapplied to Western Kentucky and started back in January 1965. I had no scholarship. This time a check for $115 from the Marine Reserves, my final mustering-out pay, provided my ticket to school. Once on campus, I immediately tried out for the track team.

But once again I encountered a coach who didn't like me. I think he decided the first day that I couldn't ever make anything of myself as a person or a runner. He told me this often enough. He made his assistant coach put me through every possible kind of workout, but I kept at it. I determined that no matter how hard he worked me, I'd show him.

One day he decided (so I found out later) to work me for four solid hours. He figured that this would make me drop out of everything. He made me do forty repeat 220s, twenty repeat 440s and twelve repeat 880s. (That means that I would run 220 yards, jog another 220, and run 220 yards again—forty times—fast, then slow; fast, then slow.) In addition, I had to finish off by running the length of the playing field forty times. He made sure that I had no real recovery time between dashes. But I kept on.

Afterward, the assistant coach told me, "You've just completed the hardest workout I've ever seen any human endure."

He told thc coach that he was wrong about me, but it did no good. That coach didn't like me and wasn't about to change.

When school resumed in the fall, our cross-country team consisted of top runners who had just graduated from high school. We all had to compete in time trials.

On one particular day, we did interval running on a golf course. That meant half a mile at top speed followed by a slow jog for the same distance, then another fast half mile until we finished five miles.

This was my senior year. It would be my last big chance to prove myself as a collegiate runner. I had trained hard all summer with my friend Jack Mahurin just for this. In those days it was unheard of for runners to work out all summer. Most of them stayed off the track from spring until fall practice.

As I ran I realized that I was keeping pace with the top runners. I knew then that I could compete with the best. We were on the twelfth 880 with times varying between 2:05 minutes and 2:10. I felt so full of life and excited. No matter what the coach threw at me, I knew I could do it.

Nearing the end of the workout, I looked over at the runner beside me. We had been kidding all along. We had already decided that we would kick it out for the last fifty yards.

"I can beat you, Mike!" I said.

"Just try!"

Both of us sprinted all out for that last few yards. Just then, the coach ran out from behind a tree, and hit me across the chest. The impact knocked me down and I lay sprawled on the ground.

In a daze, I looked up at him, hardly believing what had happened.

"You're through, Cottrell!" he said. "I won't have you running with this team again!"

I started to argue, but I knew it wouldn't do any good. He had finally won. I walked off the golf course. Later, friends encouraged me to sue him, but I never did.

During my senior year my grades were largely above average, except for a required math course. I ended up taking that course five times! I failed the first three go-rounds but by then I knew not only all the questions, but the answers as well. The fourth time I carried a 96-point average, but the instructor failed me. "You're just a smart aleck," she said, "and I base your final grade on more than just your test grades."

My cockiness had revealed itself because I constantly raised my hand to answer every question. And why not? I had taken the course so many times I didn't even have to study. The fifth time I kept quiet, passed with a high grade and finally finished with my math classes.

I had majored in physical education with a minor in both sociology and biology. During my last semester I did student teaching, carried two night classes, and worked from ten at night until seven in the morning. I even worked for a while on the assembly line at a carburetor factory. I was tired much of the time, but I was determined to make it through.

Then came graduation for the class of 1966. I wanted to make it a great event. What spare time I had, I spent walking around the campus and the town picking up soft drink bottles. The grocery store paid three cents a bottle. I wanted to give my parents a special night with a dinner that spared no expense. Then I wanted them to attend graduation ceremonies with me.

With great enthusiasm I reserved a table at one of the best restaurants in Bowling Green. Everything was set. I knew they'd enjoy every minute. At least two weeks before graduation, I had written home, telling them that I had a special dinner planned. I wrote once after that, again mentioning the dinner before going to graduation ceremonies.

But I didn't hear from my parents. That didn't surprise me, but I assumed they'd be there in plenty of time to eat. I waited around all afternoon, but they still didn't come.

Finally, at 7:00 P.M. I called home. It was at least an hour and a half's drive so if I got no answer it would at least assure me they were on the way.

After the second ring, my mother picked up the phone. My heart sank and I hardly knew how to speak to her.

"This is Stan. Aren't you coming to my graduation?"

"No, son," she said, and hesitated. "Guess we're not."

"But I planned. . . ."

"Your daddy's too tired. He's already gone to bed."

I know we talked a little more, but I don't remember anything after hearing those words: "Your daddy's too tired. He's already gone to bed."

"But I worked so hard getting ready for this," I kept saying.

"I know you're disappointed," she said, "and I'm disappointed too."

"But Momma. . . ."

"Like I said, son, your daddy's just so tired."

I never even considered asking Momma why she hadn't come. According to our Kentucky code it was unthinkable for womenfolks to be seen without their menfolks. Mother had no choice.

I was the first Cottrell to graduate from college. My mother had only completed tenth grade herself. I had worked so hard to make both of them proud of me. As I hung up the phone, a wave of despair swept over me. Didn't he know how important this was to me? Couldn't he understand how much it would have meant for me to have him present? My one chance to make him proud of my accomplishments and he wouldn't even come to see me graduate.

In my mind I had walked across that platform hundreds of times to receive my diploma. I imagined myself looking down at my parents, sitting in the audience, clapping and smiling. Daddy could have made that the most memorable night of my life. But he went to bed instead.

By the next morning I had recovered. I made all kinds of excuses for him the night before. But I faced one fact, too. Daddy had not changed. He would never change. No matter what I did he would always be ashamed of me, I thought. Realizing this only made me resolve inwardly: *I'll show you, Daddy! I'll show you that I can make something out of myself. You'll see!*

A few days later I returned to Munfordville, the disappointment already behind me. Daddy hadn't come to the graduation, but I had my diploma in my hand so that I could show him the first thing. I ran inside, eagerly waving it.

"Got my degree!" I said, and shoved it at them.

Momma smiled, obviously pleased.

Daddy didn't even look at it. "Making any money?" he said, his voice gruff.

"Well, no. . . . "

"Otherwise," he continued, "a college degree ain't worth much."

I felt my heart sink. I had wanted him to be proud of me. I had only wanted a few words of praise.

Momma said, "Oh, son, I'm proud of you. I've always known you could do anything you set your mind to." Momma usually seemed to know what to say to boost me up. But this time her words didn't help. I had already known she was proud of me. I only wanted to hear a few kind words from Daddy.

"Yeah, well, that's real nice," he said, "but you ain't no guest. You belong here and we got a farm to run. Get on your overall britches. We got work to do."

He walked out of the house. Momma looked down at her bare feet. His words hurt her, too, but she would never speak against him.

I stood in the room for a moment, in complete shock. I know now that it shouldn't have devastated me. He was only acting the way he always had. But it hurt, perhaps more than at any other time in my life. I had tried so hard to please him and to win his approval. I thought of all the extra jobs I had done, and the going without clothes and not having fun times like my classmates. I thought of the times I had studied until I fell asleep. I had scrimped every way I knew how for five years. When I'd start to get discouraged, I'd think of Daddy looking at my diploma, admiring it, and saying something like, "I'm proud of you." But he didn't say those words. Not then. Not ever.

I hurried back to my old room to change clothes, dropped my diploma on the bed and pushed my suitcase aside. It was as though I had never gone anywhere. I remember standing there, clenching my fists, wanting to run after him and scream, "What do I have to do to get your approval?" But I couldn't do that. My pride wouldn't let me.

I couldn't change him, but I wouldn't give up either. "I'll show you," I growled under my breath. "I won't give up. Nothing will stop me! Someday I'll show you!"

Right then I wanted to be ten years old so that I could at least scream and cry as loud and as long as I wanted to. But I was twenty-three.

And twenty-three-year old men don't cry.

6
"Cottrells Never 'Mit"

I've always wished that I could learn my lessons the easy way. I seldom have. Most of the time I've had to learn from my mistakes, falling down, picking myself up, and starting again. Maybe that's how most of us learn the important lessons we don't forget.

Back in my high school days in Cub Run, I got to know some of the old gentlemen who would sit in the Munfordville courthouse yard and pass the time of day by whittling. We even called them "The Non-sweat Whittlers' Club." One of these men said to me one day, "I reckon, the best way to get learnt, is you hafta get burnt." I found out what he meant when I began running long distances, over several days. I made every possible mistake.

My first attempt to run across Kentucky was one of those times.

My friend Jack Mahurin and I determined to run the distance together. We began at 5:00 A.M. on August 13, 1966, the summer after graduation. Starting at the Second Street Bridge over the Ohio River in Louisville, we planned to run the entire 146 miles across the state to the Tennessee border in two days. It was not only a great challenge, but an unheard-of event.

"You're plumb crazy," more than one person told us.

"Why you want to run that far?" another person asked.

"You mean run all the way? Every step of the way?" one woman asked.

"Yes, ma'am," I said, "Jack and I plan to run every step of the way and we plan to do it in two days."

She walked away, shaking her head.

When I told Daddy, he stared at me for a few seconds, and then walked away. I had no idea what he was thinking.

Despite what people said, however, Jack and I planned the run. We had it all worked out. The first day we would go seventy miles which would take us right to Munfordville. We'd spend the night there and then complete the remaining seventy-six miles the next day.

I don't think it occurred to either of us that we couldn't do it. Jack and I had become friends on the track team at college, based primarily on our mutual love for running. A Kentuckian from Grayson County, Jack stood six feet tall and weighed 135 pounds. Today Jack holds a PhD and teaches exercise physiology at Mississippi State University in Starkville. In 1973 he placed twelfth in the Boston Marathon. He's a champion runner—then and now.

"We can do it," I told Jack. "I just know we can."

Jack, as enthusiastic about challenges as I, agreed.

I don't know where we first got the idea of running 146 miles, but once the idea was planted in our minds, both of us knew we'd never be happy until we had done it.

A crowd of people gathered at the bridge to see us off. Many of them obviously came out of curiosity because the Louisville *Courier-Journal*, the state's largest paper, had run a feature article on us, tagging us the "Durable Duo."

We started out at exactly 5:00 A.M. And we did everything wrong!

First, we didn't take the weather into account. The day we ran, the temperature hit 96°, one of the hottest days of the year.

Second, we weren't fit for that kind of distance. Even though we both ran ten miles a day, that wasn't enough preparation. That projected distance meant that we would run the equivalent of five and a half marathons in just two days. Most people need at least a week to recuperate from *one* marathon. We were better than most runners, but we were nowhere near prepared for that kind of physical test.

Our third mistake involved equipment. In 1966 the shoe companies had not yet designed lightweight running shoes. Most shoes were made of leather and leather doesn't "breathe" as today's shoes do. The shoes caused our feet to swell and blisters to form.

We didn't wear socks either. In those days, jocks looked upon sock-wearing runners as sissies. Being tough and fit, we wore nothing inside our shoes.

Fourth, we drank the wrong thing. Not knowing any better, we filled ourselves with a milk-base supplement, loaded with vitamins. We should have been taking in a lot of water and/or diluted apple juice. Water and diluted apple juice is absorbed quickly; milk requires hours to digest. We depleted ourselves of needed body fluids by running the long distance in hot, humid weather; we were already in a state of dehydration before the milk-base liquid was absorbed.

Fifth, we made the mistake almost all novice runners make—we started out too fast. I knew it, but I didn't know how to slow down. But Jack and I were so hyped up that we gave the initial stages of the run all we had, using up energy faster than we could replace it.

We completed the first twenty-six miles in just under three hours, which gave us an average of less than seven minutes a mile. That's not bad for a marathon, but for an ultramarathon run, it's sheer stupidity.

We did one thing right. We persuaded Paul Jordan, a friend and fraternity brother, to follow us in Jack's 1965 VW. This was precautionary. We didn't want cars running us down without seeing us. Over the years runners have been hit from behind by motorists who didn't see them in time to stop. The VW trailed us, displaying a sign, TENNESSEE ON FOOT OR BUST. With Paul behind us we did not worry about traffic creeping up on us. Our friend also carried a first-aid kit of tape, Band-Aids and petroleum jelly.

Forty miles out of Louisville, as we neared Fort Knox, we ran into highway construction. We could pass but our feet took a beating as we pounded the gravel and uneven surfaces. By then, I think Jack and I were both beginning to realize that we couldn't make such a run in two days. My feet were already swelling and I felt as if they would burst through my leather shoes.

By the time we reached Elizabethtown, fifty-five miles from

Louisville, we were finished. Jack groaned every time he lifted a foot. Somewhere after the start Jack had been smart enough to put on socks, which helped cushion against the shocks and blisters. But his knees did him in.

Finally, Jack stopped and so did I. He had more sense than I. He was ready to call it off. But something in me wouldn't quit. Then Daddy's pickup truck appeared out of nowhere. He honked once, and motioned for me to come over. I was totally amazed. I hadn't expected to see him there—we were thirty miles from Munfordville, at least. Yet down deep inside, the little boy in me was glad to see my dad.

Looking back on it now, I realize that Daddy never could express his approval of me in words. Yet, in his own paradoxical way, he was concerned. Later I learned that he had followed me most of the way.

But I didn't think about Daddy then. I hurt all over, especially my feet. They were swollen so badly and the slightest movement sent sharp pains shooting through my legs.

"Daddy, call me a doctor. Get me a prescription for morphine," I begged.

He shook his head, "Nosirree."

"Just get in," he said, leaning over to open the pickup door.

"I can't. I've still got fifteen miles to run. I can't quit now."

He stared at me a second as if he had no idea what to say.

"Daddy, I'm hurting. Just a little morphine will do it—"

He shook his head. "You've run fifty-five miles, son. That's honorable."

That is as close as he could come to saying, "I'm proud of what you've done today." But I really didn't hear him then. At the moment I only wanted to finish those last fifteen miles. Despite all the pain, I couldn't give up.

"You did great!" somebody behind me yelled.

"How many other people in the world can run fifty-five miles in a single day?" a friend said as he slapped my shoulder.

People grouped around me, patting me on the back and congratulating me. I didn't hear their words as sounds of victory, only as consolation for defeat.

"Daddy, please," I begged, ignoring all the excitement around me, hardly aware of what they were saying. Tears streamed down my cheeks because of the pain. I couldn't stop them. I hurt so badly that I couldn't think of anything except getting some relief so that I could finish up my last fifteen miles. Daddy sat there acting as if he hadn't heard me. I kept pleading. "If I can get an injection in my feet, you know, like novacaine works on the mouth, then I can go on and finish this run. Please, Daddy, I can't give up now."

I hurt so badly I couldn't reason properly. Even though I knew I sounded crazy I couldn't quit begging.

Every time I looked away from my father I saw that sign, TENNESSEE ON FOOT OR BUST. Fresh tears stung my eyes and I decided that, pain or not, I would start running again.

Daddy must have read the determination in my eyes because he said simply, "Get in the truck, son."

I didn't want to get into that pickup. I wanted to scream back at him, "No! I'm going on!" But, being brought up by the code of the hills, even at my age I didn't argue with my father. Obediently I hobbled over to the pickup and got inside, trying not to let the pain fill my thoughts.

Later, when Momma peeled my shoes and socks from my swollen feet, we saw that I had lost six toenails. For a few days, we feared that the doctor might have to amputate the little toe on my left foot. It took weeks before I could wear regular shoes again.

"Stanley junior, how you feeling?" an old high school buddy asked.

"Just great—from the knees up," I said, glad that my sense of humor hadn't failed.

But it seemed as if I had failed in just about every other way. I had told the world, and especially Daddy, that I would run across the entire state. I had started, but I hadn't finished. Even though all my friends told me what a great race I had run, I found no consolation in that. I had let my daddy down. I had promised and then failed. Daddy wasn't a quitter and he had trained me never to quit.

When I was a boy, Daddy used to wrestle with my brother Harold and me. He would get me down, pull my arm up behind me and hold it until it started to hurt, and then say, "Do you 'mit? Do you 'mit?" And if I said yes, Daddy would answer, "No you can't, because Cottrells never 'mit!" (Cottrells never submit.)

I remember Daddy getting a hammerlock on Harold and holding it for thirty or forty minutes. All of the time Harold would be screaming and crying.

"Do you 'mit?" Daddy would ask him.

"No!" Harold would holler, even though he thought he was going to die.

"Why?" Daddy would ask.

"'Cause Cottrells never 'mit!"

Finally Daddy would let him go. This would happen over and over while we were growing up. We had a sore arm for a week after one of these encounters with Daddy. But one thing stuck in our souls—*Cottrells never 'mit.*

The next day after our failed run across Kentucky, the *Courier-Journal* carried a follow-up story: "Tennessee on Foot or Bust, Busted."

I had failed. Cottrells never 'mit. But I had no choice. I had learned some things from that defeat. For one thing, I had been too idealistic. I assumed that simply because I had set a goal I could achieve it by sheer willpower. From then on when I planned a run I tried to take into consideration everything that could possibly go wrong.

I learned that setting goals involves paying a price. Nothing worthwhile ever comes free or without effort. I often say it this way:

> If there's going to be addition in life, there must first be subtraction.

For me, to achieve long distances as a runner meant giving up several things. I had to determine my priorities. I didn't go to the parties and enjoy many fun times with my friends. Because of the heavy physical demands for stamina and strength, I learned about nutrition, and to avoid greasy foods and soft drinks, the diet of most college young people. While my friends cruised around town or dated, I was on the road running.

I also paid the price in isolation. Because I ran so much, most people didn't understand me and I had long given up trying to explain. Sometimes I wondered, *Why can't I be like other people? Why am I different?* It took at least another fifteen years before I could answer my own questions.

Had I been given a choice to do anything I wanted, I would have chosen running. If anyone was ever born to run, it must be Stanley Cottrell, Jr. Running satisfies a lot of needs in me. At that time I knew that running provided comfort in the midst of rejection and tension. Running long distances became my time to dream of what could happen in my life.

But in the 1960s people didn't run for a career. They might coach track in high school or college, or train for Olympic competition, but that was the end of it. It never occurred to me to be a runner as an occupation.

Up to my senior year in college my major goal had been to get off the farm and never to return. But during my senior year I gave a lot of thought to a new goal—earning a living.

In those days it seemed that most people who attended college ended up being teachers. That is, with the exception of a few professions, like medicine and law. So, it was natural for me to think, almost automatically, that I should go into teaching. The more I thought about this, the more this burned within me as my vocational goal. I would teach and I would also coach track. Fortunately for me, I had taken enough of the right courses to certify me as a teacher in biology and health.

Would I make a good teacher and coach? I believed I would, because of one special instructor I had trained under in college.

During my senior year I had done my required practice teaching under the supervision of Coach Ed Brannon. White-haired and a muscular two hundred pounds, Mr. Brannon stood six feet tall. He coached football and, although he smiled and joked a lot, he knew how to get tough when necessary.

On the third day of my practice teaching I was telling Coach Brannon all about the bell curve as if he had never heard of it before. "It's really ingenious," I said. "You can fairly well predict that out of any class, approximately 22 percent of the students will be in the A and B categories, and approximately the same number will be below average to failure. . . . "

"That so?" he interrupted.

"Sure is," and I showed him the graphs and figures I had made up for the class. I had everyone analyzed and statistically projected so that I could show how I could predict which students fell into the fast-, medium-, or slow-learning categories.

When I handed him a large chart on which I had worked nearly twelve hours, he glanced at it, and threw it aside. "Stan, I want to tell you something," he said. "These kids we teach aren't a bell curve. They're just human beings. Treat them that way."

His attitude shocked me. After all, I was only using the tools given me in college.

"That stuff," he said, and pushed the chart aside a second time, "is worth nothing unless you first remember that they're human beings. They aren't figures on a graph."

"I didn't mean that. . . . "

"You have to relate to them, Stan. When those students know you're a human being, that's the first day you become a teacher. *Then* you can sit down and make your graphs and draw up your charts. Then you can fiddle around with blue, red, green, or whatever colors you want to indicate anything. But don't do it until you know them as people."

Coach Brannon had been teaching almost as long as I had been alive. For once I had the good sense to shut up and thank him for what he said. I never forgot his words either. He taught me one of the most valuable lessons of life—people come first. "Don't forget the human element."

7
Charlene Was the Kind Men Looked At

In September 1966, I took a job as a cross-country coach in Louisville, Kentucky. I had filled out sixty-five applications while practice teaching and had received sixty-four offers.

Trouble for me started from the first day in Louisville. All of 23 years old, blond, fair-skinned, and looking as young as some of the high school students, I probably did not impress the principal very much. He seemed to take a protective and fatherly attitude toward me.

"I want to help you, Mr. Cottrell," he said. "You're new and young. . . . " Then followed a brief lecture on the greatness of the teaching profession. Abruptly he stopped, as if he had just thought of it, and said, "By the way, have you found a place to stay yet?"

"No, sir, I just got into town."

"Tell you what to do," he said, and scribbled on a piece of paper. "You go over to this address. It's my wife's mother. She's got a nice room. It's near the school and reasonable. You'll like it there." He gave me directions and said he'd call her.

I went to the house and it was quite nice. "Looks like I'll enjoy Louisville," I remember saying to myself. And after looking over the room and hearing the price, I told the landlady that I would take it.

She smiled—for the first time. "Oh, and there are just a few rules I have around here. Nothing much, but a few things I insist upon."

"Sure, as long as they're reasonable, why not?" I said, not having any idea of what she meant by a few rules.

She wore glasses that slipped down to the tip of her nose. She constantly peered over them. "You have a radio in your room. You may play it until nine P.M. After that, it goes off. If you want guests, you may use the parlor—" which she showed me. "But your friends must be gone by 9:30." She laid down another ten or twelve rules.

"What?" I finally asked. "Are you serious?"

"Absolutely," she said, and started on another rule.

"Ma'am," I said, picking up my single suitcase, "I don't think I'll stay here after all. Thank you just the same." I didn't explain or try to argue. I just walked out. I had no intention of living a wild sort of life, but I also decided I was an adult. I had been away from home before. I didn't need another mother and I sure didn't need a drill instructor either. After working hard for my college degree, I didn't need a lot of petty rules worse than those of the university.

Naturally the principal didn't like it, although he tried to be kind about it. I should have understood then that he wasn't going to forget what I had done in rejecting all of his good intentions.

As the fall semester began, he constantly found ways to harass me. If he could find a way to embarrass me in front of the other teachers, he did that too. He finally decided mainly on one ploy.

"Mr. Cottrell, please report to the principal's office," boomed the secretary's voice over the loudspeaker and throughout the whole school. This became a morning ritual.

By the second week, kids snickered when they heard the message. Somehow the word had gotten around school about what happened. Each morning we went through almost the same game. I was cocky, pleased with myself over having a degree, and not about to let anyone else run my life.

"You seem to be paying a lot of attention to the girls," the principal said, "or so it seems to me. As you well know, teacher-student relationships are forbidden. And they *are* minors. . . . "

After the third week, I finally said, "Look, judge me by my teaching and by my behavior, *not* by what your dirty mind thinks I'm doing."

"I know what's going on in your dirty mind, Mr. Cottrell. I see the way you look at those girls."

Those morning sessions in his office kept up. He managed to ruin every morning for me and I saw no end in sight. I wasn't going to buckle under either.

I coached the boys in cross-country running and spent a lot of time with them outside of class. I became one of them. Not only did I coach them on how to run; I moved right along beside them. It became a challenge to most of them to outdistance me on two- and three-mile runs. They seldom did, but they always kept trying in a kind of friendly rivalry.

It became common knowledge that I spent time with my students away from the track. Although we had no rule against it, other teachers let me know that one of the unwritten policies is that we keep a sharp line of distinction between students and teachers.

That fall, the students chose the ten most popular teachers. Even though I was new, I received 45 percent of the votes. A few days after the announcement of the ten most popular teachers, the Optimist Club contacted me. They had heard about my work with the students and wanted to recognize my efforts. I had a genuine feeling that I could succeed as a coach and a teacher.

However, as much as I enjoyed this recognition, I had enough sense to know that the antagonism between the principal and me would only increase. So, I contacted a school in Michigan, was accepted, and arrived there at the end of November.

In Michigan I met Charlene and began a new phase in my life. Charlene was the kind of girl men looked at—and continued to look at. Even women commented, "Isn't she beautiful?" She had blue eyes and blond hair. Maybe that's why I felt so overwhelmed when she found herself attracted to me.

I was twenty-three years old, teaching in Michigan, and one of the few unmarried teachers on the staff. Three other teachers and I were assigned to chaperone a junior-senior prom.

Charlene, who had graduated the previous year, and whom I had never met, saw me and thought I was one of the seniors. She had come to the dance with several of her friends, but after a while she left them, walked up to me with a full smile, cocked her head and said, "Well, you just going to stand there or are you going to dance with me?" She smiled in a way that made me feel as if I were not only special, but that for the moment, I was the only boy in the world.

"Me?" I said, because it had not occurred to me that I would dance. After all, I was there to chaperone. I glanced toward the other chaperones and they giggled. One of them nodded as if to say, "Go ahead and dance."

"Well, are you going to dance with her?" the other asked.

I looked at Charlene again as she said, "Well?"

"I—I guess so."

I took her arm and we moved onto the floor. The band played a slow number and I held myself as far away from her as possible. Being a teacher and a chaperone, I didn't want to give any wrong impression to anyone there.

"What's the matter with you?" Charlene asked. "Why can't you dance right?"

I knew what she meant, of course, but I asked, "What's wrong?"

"You dancing with me or someone across the room?"

I moved a little closer, but stayed far enough away so that no one would possibly think that anything was going on between us. I determined to keep the right image in front of the students. I still felt awkward.

"Loosen up," she said a couple of times, "and come a little closer."

I smiled and came even a little closer, still not knowing what to do. Out of the corner of my eyes, I saw other couples plastered together, which was the style during those kinds of dances.

"Hey, look at the teach," someone said from behind me.

"Go! Go! Go!"

"Teach, whatcha doing there?" another voice called. I knew they were delighted to see me on the floor, because I had already developed a good relationship with them.

Charlene looked into my eyes. "Oh, you're a teacher? I didn't know," she said. "I thought you were nineteen at the most."

"Does it make any difference?" I asked. "Being older doesn't help me dance any better."

She laughed, and that broke the strain. I still didn't hold her close, but at least she understood.

We danced two or three more times and I found the conversation had grown easy and natural. I forgot about my role as chaperone and enjoyed being with this attractive girl.

"I'm here with several of my friends who are seniors," she said. "After the dance we're all going out to a place for fun and food. Want to come along?"

"I can't really do that," I said.

"Sure you can."

"I'm a chaperone—and I could get into trouble—"

"Aw, okay," she said, and pouted. "Big, bad teacher can't come."

She left then and started to walk away. Then she turned back and said, "You know, you're real bold." *Bold* was the *in* word in those days that covered the expressions we'd use today such as, "you're a hunk, you're good looking."

I flushed, hardly knowing what to say. It wasn't until later that I understood what she meant. "I'm bold?" I repeated.

Seeing my embarrassment, she said, "Now you're cute. And I like that. You're okay."

"You think so?" I managed to say, flattered that such a beautiful girl would say those words to me. And, not having dated much in college, I didn't feel comfortable.

We chatted a few more minutes and then she said, "Tell you what. Let's just forget about where the kids are all going. I'd just like to see you."

I had never been exposed to such openness in a woman before. I had come from the Kentucky hills and lived by the code of those hills which said that men make the choices and pursue women. "Uh, well, okay," I mumbled. "It's okay with me."

"Are all Kentucky people like you?" she asked, and it sounded so flattering.

I couldn't believe that such a gorgeous person could be attracted to me. Other than one or two girls at home like Beth, females hadn't been particularly anxious to go out with me. I mixed well with people and could always keep parties alive. Yet at the same time, the inner me shied away from deep contact or commitment to a person. I think I feared that Charlene would not find me so attractive once she got to know me well.

As I write about Charlene it may sound as if she came on strong, but I saw it as more of a friendly challenge than anything else. And I loved it. Although younger, she epitomized glamor, fun in life, and a sample of that big world outside of Kentucky that I wanted to grab hold of.

While wanting to be with her, I couldn't believe that my southern ways appealed to her or that she actually wanted to go out with me. Yet Charlene did. That night led to a date the next night and then to more dates. We spent time together but we never talked in depth. I was lured by her looks. Just being with her was enough.

Once in a while I tried to talk on a deeper level, asking questions such as, "What's life all about? I'd like to know who I am."

She would listen politely and say, "Do you always think that deep?" Somehow that put an end to the introspection.

At times I would feel frustrated because we couldn't talk about the real issues of life. I didn't know exactly what I wanted in life, but I had a gnawing desire for success and felt that I'd never be happy until I conquered whatever it took to reach the top.

We met in November 1966 at the dance the first week I began teaching in Michigan. And we were married the following summer. That same summer I transferred to a school in Florida. I couldn't take the cold of those Michigan winters. (The last snow that year was in April. I didn't want to go through that again.) We were both young and Charlene, always full of adventure, agreed to the transfer without the slightest hesitation.

With my Camaro that I just "had" to have, we drove to Florida. I was able to rent government-subsidized housing in Orange Park; our apartment rented for $40 a month. We had a hundred dollars when we moved in, but no furniture. But that didn't seem to bother either of us. We made pallets on the floor and slept that way for several weeks.

People couldn't believe we were as old as we were. Several times during the three years I taught at the school, little articles appeared in the school newspaper about us. They idealized us as the clean-cut, sweet couple, both of whom looked sixteen years old.

We did look like sixteen-year-olds, a fact that made us a hit among the young people. But we also acted like sixteen-year-olds. That would cause severe problems later on.

8
From Teacher—to Salesman—to Single Parent

One of the best things that came out of our time in Florida was meeting George and Maxine Boatwright. Their son ran on the cross-country track team I coached.

"I'd like you to meet my parents," George Boatwright, Jr., said one day. "How about coming by for supper? You and your wife?"

"Sure, why not?" I said, always glad to have a home-cooked meal and a chance to meet new people. Charlene loved the idea.

When George junior and I walked up to the house, I saw the shock on his parents' faces. "You—you must be one of the boys from. . . ."

"No, ma'am," I said, "I'm Stan Cottrell, George junior's coach."

George and Maxine went into gales of laughter. Their son hadn't described me but they expected a tall, middle-aged man with broad shoulders and long legs. Instead they saw this slightly-under-medium-tall blond with boyish features. I wore a baseball cap, T-shirt, jeans, and shoes with no socks.

Seconds later, Charlene ran up to the house. They could easily have mistaken her for George junior's classmate too. She wore a tight-fitting blouse, shorts, and sandals.

"Guess we weren't expecting to find two kids at our door."

We all laughed. They didn't intend any insult with their words, just an honest admission of the situation. That's one of the first qualities I liked about the Boatwrights: they were up front about how they felt, and very warm inside.

They took us into their hearts. For as long as we lived in Orange Park, they were our special friends. Actually, they functioned more like parents than friends, which was good. Both of us needed a lot of help in adjusting to marriage. They patiently taught us almost everything because I knew nothing about being a husband, let alone being a parent.

Parenthood came, nine months and twenty minutes after the marriage ceremony. We named her Michelle. Neither of us even knew how to change a diaper or what to do when the baby cried. Had it not been for the Boatwrights I don't think we could have survived.

They taught us how to manage money. When we moved to Florida, we made no use of common sense, bought what we saw, and never thought seriously about how we would pay. I was bringing home $325.00 a month. On paper it seemed as though it would go a long way. But not the way we spent it.

I bought on credit, with terms such as ten dollars a month on a refrigerator, another fifteen dollars for a stereo. I had skimped and scraped for years and now I thought I could have everything I wanted. I was like a blind dog in a meat house, grabbing for everything I could. I had overextended myself to the point that the finance company repossessed my car during the first six months of marriage.

Yet we took it all in stride. We didn't worry much, figuring we could always work things out. And somehow we did. For instance, I met a multi-millionaire who lived in the area. He had bought a VW bus simply to take his garbage the full mile from his house to the end of his driveway where the city collected it twice a week. He offered me a wonderful deal. In exchange for my picking up his garbage on Sunday and Wednesday, and carrying it to the end of the driveway, he gave us full use of his bus.

I also learned about how to eat when we had no money. George discovered and told me that the local A & P threw away their produce on Saturday after closing. Later each Saturday I drove over and picked up items such as wilted lettuce or the black-flecked bananas that would be spoiled by Monday. That provided the staples for the next week.

George Boatwright taught me how to cast a net for mullet. At least once a week we had fresh fish on our table. George also had a relative who owned a potato farm. Several times we drove over to the fields, dug up potatoes, and stored them in George's garage. Had it not been for the Boatwrights, I have no idea how we would have made it through that first year.

Charlene and I got burnt a few times—mainly because I had no idea how to manage money. The pay scale didn't help. By my fourth year of teaching I grossed $6,215.00, including pay for teaching during summer school and my coaching supplement. My monthly take-home pay came to a grand total of $375. I decided to supplement my income and took a night job cooking at a fast food restaurant. When school officials heard about it, they were horrified.

"You're a teacher. An example to this community!"

"It's honest work," I said, "and I need the money."

"I'm sure we can help you some other way," the principal said, still shaking his head, hardly believing that I would lower myself. Actually I never thought of it like that. I needed the money and it was the only kind of job I could think of holding down with my hectic schedule. I wasn't ashamed of work.

Later I realized that the school officials felt it was a black mark against the system. As a coach I had a lot of visibility in the community. They didn't want it thought that their teachers had to demean themselves.

The next thing I knew I had a part-time job in a junior college, teaching adult education. The principal had come through for me, but I panicked. I ran over to my friends for help.

"George, I don't know anything about teaching psychology," I groaned. "I'm glad for the chance, but I don't know what to teach them." George had majored in psychology in the University of Florida. In simple steps, he laid out the lesson for me. Each week, I studied the material, then went to George. In two hours, he planned it all out and coached me on how to present it. That year I received all kinds of praise for my classroom work at the junior college. I owed it all to George who, in his quiet, slow-moving way, taught me how to teach others.

Thirteen months after Michelle's birth, Stanley Cottrell, III, was born. But this time it didn't take me forty-five minutes to change a diaper. Charlene and I had become experts, but we still depended on the Boatwrights for coaching us in other things.

Charlene and I involved ourselves in a local church. She taught 13-year-old girls and I had the teenaged boys. Eventually I became superintendent of the youth department. Even though we were active in the church, we never talked about God or about our faith, at least not seriously.

Maybe that should have worried me, but it didn't. Even after two years of marriage, I don't think Charlene really understood me. I certainly didn't understand her. I loved her. She fascinated me. She enjoyed life and always opened herself to new experiences. I tended to hold back.

With the passage of time I realize that we had built our relationship upon the superficial things in life: physical attraction, having a good time, living new adventures. But we never talked about things in depth. On the few occasions when I still tried to talk seriously, she would flash that dazzling smile and her lips would pout slightly. "Oh, Stanley," she'd say. That would end the discussion. We lived together, but we didn't think and share together. We never talked seriously about many things.

One thing we did manage to talk about during those days was our lack of money—and that teaching didn't offer much of a future. The only thing I could look forward to in the way of increased financial security, if I remained in education, was administration. And I did not want that.

We didn't live extravagantly. But even when we tried to economize, providing for a family of four meant we never had quite enough to pay all the bills and still have anything left over.

The parents of several of my students were in sales and they frequently would call and say, "We've heard enthusiastic reports about you. We'd like to talk to you about a job with us."

"You'd be terrific," they would say. "You could easily learn anything more you need to know. . . ."

"There's no limit to what you make in sales," said one friend. "A man with your ability can go places." That sort of talk finally got me to leave the teaching profession.

Most every day I was running at least ten miles. And as I did, I kept thinking about those job possibilities in sales. I enjoyed teaching and especially liked working with young people. I hated the thought of leaving the teenagers. But then I realized that each year several of them graduated anyway.

While I ran, pictures filled my mind. I dreamed of having a nice home for Char and our two children. I envisioned what it would be like to have a good balance in the bank after the bills were paid. The words of friends would come back to me: "There's no limit to what you make. . . ." "A man with your ability can go places. . . ." Such encouragement fed my ego and stimulated that drive for success—that inner need to achieve and to rise above the average.

One day a close friend said, "Stan, you'd make a great detail man." I didn't even know what a detail man was. He explained that a detail man sold pharmaceuticals by personally going to doctors and introducing their new products. In short, a drug salesman.

After several weeks, I made up my mind. During the Christmas holidays George Boatwright helped me compose a letter and write a resumé. The friend who had suggested that I would make a great detail man contacted thirty-five pharmaceutical companies. They all set up interviews with me and most of them later offered me a job. I finally narrowed it down to the L. R. Squibb Company. But in taking the job, we had to move from Jacksonville to Savannah, Georgia. We hated leaving the Boatwrights, but the opportunity to achieve success excited us both. We had lived in the protected environment of George and Maxine long enough.

The new job scared me. I didn't know anything about drugs. I could hardly pronounce the names of most of them and had no idea what doctors used them for. Not having any previous experience in sales, I kept wondering if I had made a mistake.

I might never have made anything of myself as a salesman had it not been for my boss. Chuck Martin, a Tennesseean by birth, took me under his wing. He taught me and instilled confidence in me. Chuck gave me the practical tips about selling that I needed. "You've got to romance your products," he told me. "Be enthusiastic about them. Let folks know you believe in what you're selling. You need to give them a reason to buy your product." Those direct statements made sense. I listened and put that together with something more valuable than selling technique—the value of relationships.

I was learning to sell and at the same time, I continued to run. And for the first time my running had fringe benefits. Because I ran ten to twenty miles daily, people started to recognize me. In Savannah in those days there weren't many runners around, so people soon got to know me. And in true southern fashion they would greet me as I passed by.

Those casual greetings became an easy way for me to introduce myself to people as I met them on the street. "Aren't you that man who runs all over Savannah?" they would ask.

"Sure am," I'd respond, knowing they had just paid me a high compliment.

Before long we would be in conversation. Those casual meetings developed into ongoing relationships with a few. Doctors began to know about me, more as a runner than as a drug salesman. Some doctors let me see them because they wanted to know about physical exercise and running, which was just starting to become a national craze. I got several of them hooked on running. We developed social relationships and they, in turn, introduced me to other doctors.

In the beginning I didn't take advantage of those referrals. I would visit with the doctors, talk, socialize with them, and sometimes we would jog a few miles together. I would say, "By the way, there's a new product our company has come out with." I didn't push my product and never gave them a reason to buy it. My low-key approach wasn't working.

That's when the light switch went on and I decided to try it the company way. I had neglected one of Chuck's cardinal rules of selling: romance the product.

"A sale is made in the first three minutes," he had told me more than once. "You've got to get in there and make the pitch right off."

I decided to do just that on my first visit to an older physician who was a terror to most salesmen. "He'll eat you alive," one of them told me. But I was undaunted. I honestly believed in my product and couldn't wait to "make the pitch." But I did have to wait. Five long hours.

Finally the receptionist said to me, "You may see the doctor now." I followed her into the same room that dozens of patients had entered earlier in the day. Down a small hallway she led me and into his private office. There sat the doctor, hunched over his desk, wearing half-moon glasses, thrashing through a pile of papers in front of him. Without even looking up, he said in his gravelly voice, "Young man, you've got thirty seconds and ten of it's gone. Now what have you got to say?"

His words stunned me but it took only a second for me to recover. I turned and started to walk out of the door.

"Where you going?" He finally raised his eyes and looked at me.

"I can't tell you anything," I said. "Twenty seconds are already gone. I refuse to do a disservice to me and to my company with our unique products."

I reached for the door handle and as I turned around, I stopped and went back to him. I leaned across his desk so that he got a very clear look at my face. "I want to tell you something, you big old woolly bear. You and I might have been friends. That's the worst that could have come out of this meeting. But we'll never know, will we?" I turned to leave, and then looked around at him for just a moment. "But I'm gonna love you anyway," I said, and went for the door.

"Get back here!" he demanded. "Where'd you learn that approach?"

I shook my head. "I didn't learn that anywhere. It's just what I feel," I said. "I don't know your problem and I don't know why you're chewing me alive, but I know enough from basic psychology to know that underneath all your gruffness is a man who's hurting."

"Sit down," he said, and his voice took on a softness I hadn't heard before. We spent nearly an hour together, getting to know one another. I talked very little about the product that time. But a friendship was born. Over the next two years I often visited his home. He opened doors for sales for me by introducing me to other physicians, and as our friendship developed, I even helped him get into shape. As long as I remained in the Savannah area he was not only one of my best customers, but a close friend.

That was the first time I discovered a deep satisfaction in reaching out and trying to help others. By caring about him, I sold my product. But more important, I developed a relationship and both of us profited.

I knew my products. I studied hard. I spent most of my free time getting to know the products I sold. But more and more I realized that people come first. I didn't have to learn that lesson from Chuck. Coach Brannon had taught me that years earlier. Sometimes I forgot and on occasion I hustled my product to beat a record or to bring in a high sales level. But most of the time, those words from Coach Brannon stayed with me: people come first.

Everybody wants to be loved and needs others to care. By caring about my customers it also paid off in success.

While working for Squibb, I traveled a lot. I know now that it must have been hard on Charlene. She was still so young, barely twenty-one, the mother of two young kids, and trapped at home. Because of my schedule and my workaholic nature, I had little time to spend with her.

Naturally I expected Char to make friends. With her outgoing personality and natural charm, I knew she would get acquainted easily. Not that we talked much about her friends, because we didn't talk much about anything. But when we did talk, I noticed that more and more of her conversation centered around two women, what they said, what they thought, what they did. I didn't like anything she told me about them. Her relationship with those two people probably did more to drive us apart than anything. And perhaps the best way to explain those two women is simply to say that both of them and their husbands were later convicted in Georgia for drug trafficking in the eastern United States. A segment of the television program "60 Minutes" profiled them.

Eventually I met both of them and liked neither one. Right away I saw what a bad influence they were on Charlene in that they had no morals.

That night, after my meeting these women, I said to Char, "I don't want you to have anything more to do with them."

"They're fine people," she retorted.

"Honey, I've never asked you not to be involved with anyone before. But this time, I'm doing that."

"They're *my* friends," she said. "Remember, I'm stuck here all the time with two tiny kids. Besides, I like them."

"Can't you find other friends?"

"What's wrong with the ones I've got?"

"They're not the kind of people you need."

"I think I know what kind of people I need."

I paused, not wanting to argue over it, but not willing to give up either. "I don't think they're a good influence on Michelle and little Stan."

"Do I ever tell you what kind of friends to have?"

We went back and forth over this for weeks. Finally, for the sake of peace, I decided to accept them as my friends, too. "Okay, Char, I'll try to like them."

A few days later, these women invited us to a party. The address impressed me because it was a fashionable part of Savannah. The people had a large house with immense trees and shrubs, giving them privacy from the rest of the community. Inside I saw obviously expensive furnishings. During the first half of the party, I must have met twenty people. I had almost decided that I might like these people when someone lit up a marijuana cigarette.

Almost everyone had a drink in one hand. Music blared in the background; the noise level continued to rise and the drinking increased. I moved around, so that I didn't stay too long talking to any couple or individual. I didn't feel comfortable.

All of a sudden a woman, standing in full view of everyone, started peeling off her clothes. A couple of people laughed. Then a man walked over and said, "I can do that, too," and they raced to see who got undressed first.

I didn't wait to see anything more. Grabbing Char's arm, I said, "We're going!"

"They're just having fun!" she explained.

"We're going," I said. Ordinarily I didn't make that kind of demands, but I couldn't stay in that kind of place.

"Stan, I want to stay," Char resisted. But I pulled her through the crowded living room and out of the house. I didn't let go until she was inside the car.

She said only one thing to me: "You embarrassed me in front of my friends." We didn't say another word the rest of the night.

By then I realized what a totally negative influence those two women held on her. However, it was too late to fight it. They had more influence on her than the kids and I did. They said things to her (which she later repeated to me) such as, "Stan's just packing your head with crazy things. Why did you marry him in the first place?"

Arguments arose over minor things Now we not only couldn't talk seriously; we could hardly talk at all without bickering and yelling. I kept insisting that we establish relationships with people who would be *our* friends.

"Don't tell me who to choose as my friends," she would say. "I don't ever try to tell you who to like or to associate with."

The end had already begun and neither of us knew how to change or stop it. While on the road, especially in the far corners of the state, I would phone home in the evenings. More and more frequently a baby-sitter answered. Charlene put the children in a nursery during the day and hired baby-sitters at night.

Little Stan's problems became more noticeable to me in the nursery. He couldn't adjust to it and cried constantly. When I would come home I would see how miserable the children were. I would say something about it, but Charlene would either refuse to talk or would change the subject. "I wish I could get away from the kids," she said more than once. "I feel tied down all the time."

Life and Times of Stan Cottrell

· oldest sister, Mary, and I in the field on our Kentucky farm.

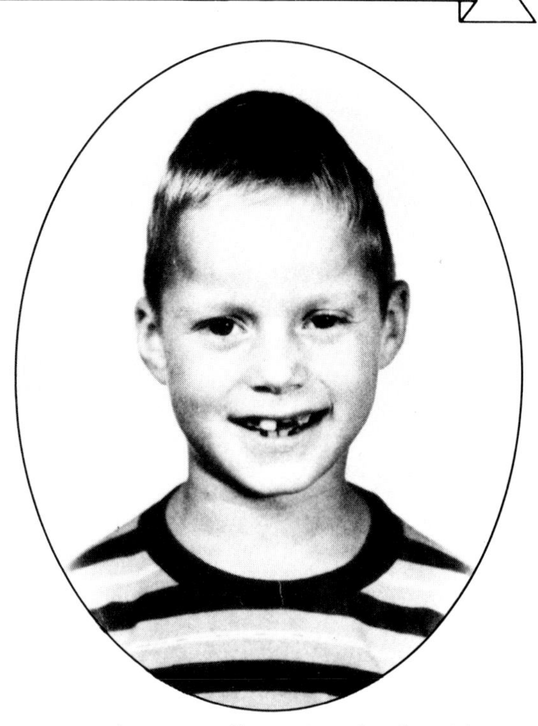

Stanley Cottrell, Jr. First Grade, 1949.

My father with his children on the Munfordville farm, about 1953. From left: Shirley, Mary, my little brother Harold on Daddy's lap, and me. Fiddler, a hound pup, is in front. Sisters Pam and Debbie were not yet born.

My first award for running—a blue ribbon for winning the 100-yard dash. I was twelve.

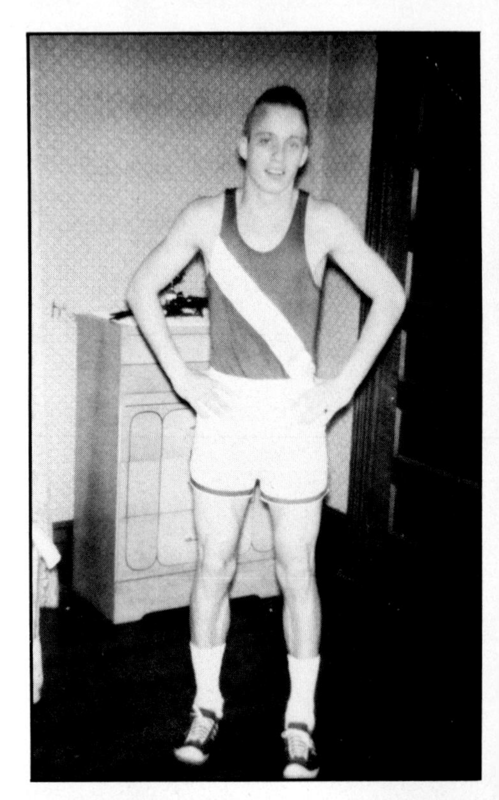

I ordered my first running outfit from the catalog, complete with shoes, for under $10. I was sixteen.

Jack Mahurin and I rest in Munfordville on our ill-fated "Tennessee or Bust on Foot" run across Kentucky. At right is Daddy; at left, Paul Jordan.

I cross the finish line in the 1964 Boston Marathon.

My first track team — Warren County (Ky.) High School, Spring 1966. Front row: Phillip Poteet, David Pickett, Forrest Hodge, Fred Mahone, Mike Osborne. Back row: Stan Cottrell, Jr., Ron Hinton, Tommy Kitchens, Donald Jones, Homer Decker, Buster Smith.

Jim Hansford of the Lung Association presents the Georgia Humanitarian Athlete of the Year award to me after my run across Georgia in 1978. My daughter Jennifer (4) joins me.

My wife Carol applies petroleum jelly to my feet during a break on my 24-hour run for the record, Sept. 25, 1979, at the Lovett School in Atlanta, Georgia.

Friends from Munfordville, including my mother, surprised me by coming to Indianapolis as I ran through the city on the Great American Friendship Run in 1980. "The good Lord will help you," Momma said.

Singer Willie Nelson ran along with me as I approached Lake Tahoe on the run across America.

How cool it is! At the Golden Gate Bridge—three thousand blistering miles after leaving New York City—I refresh my feet with champagne presented to me (left). My two strongest supporters—Carol and Momma—met me in San Francisco at the finish line, July 3, 1980 (near below). Daddy did an unforgettable thing on "Stan Cottrell Day" in Munfordville in November 1979, months before his death. A master basket weaver, he presented me with one of his finest baskets (bottom).

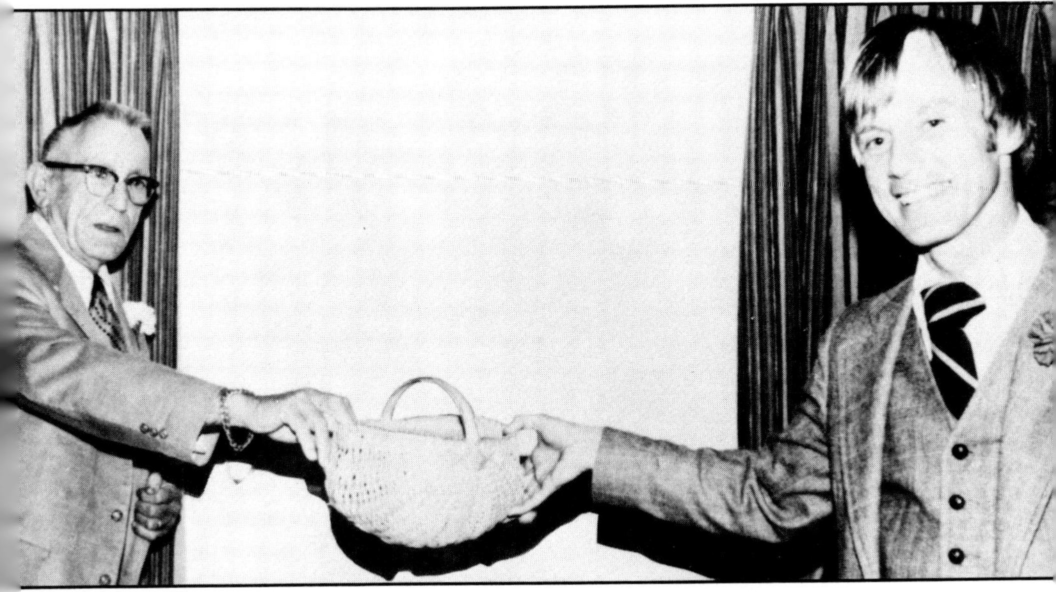

Hugo Greiner, M.D., of Decatur, Georgia, a specialist who studied sports medicine in Germany, was my trainer, companion, and photographer all the way across Europe. *(Associated Press photo, used with permission)*

To shield my hands from freezing rain in Italy, I wore plastic bags over my gloves. To shield me from the onrushing traffic, and to pace me, Dr. Greiner was always nearby on his bicycle. *(Foto Omaggio, used by permission)*

The Great European Adventure Run started in Edinburgh, Scotland. Here I am, early in the 80-day run, passing through an English city.

In Cologne, Germany, at the Institute for Circulation Research, medical people put me through rigorous tests and examinations after the run through Europe (top). At the Rock of Gibraltar, I was jubilant. The run was completed (Dec. 7, 1982); I was looking ahead to the Dominican Republic run (right).

In June 1983, following my friendship run across the Dominican Republic, I was introduced to the genuine warmth of Latin camaraderie.

Under Kansas skies, the Run for America is a battle against headwinds and blistering sun, a tough test of willpower and fitness (top). Stan and Carol Cottrell, with Michelle (top center), Stanley III and Jennifer.

"If a divorce is what you really want, all right . . . " I answered.

"I didn't say I wanted a divorce," she replied.

"You talk like you do," I said.

And then she said: "I don't know. Maybe that's what I do want."

"Char," I pleaded, "if that's what you really want, all right. Just give me custody of the kids."

"Custody?" she asked. "How could you take care of them? You're gone too much now."

"I'd find a way to work it out," I assured her. She only answered, "Oh, sure."

"You're never around anyway," I said, knowing I had hurt her. I reminded her of all the baby-sitters we hired and the constant use of the nursery.

Our voices rose in pitch and tempers flared, but at last we had gotten things into the open. After we had calmed down a little I said, "I want the responsibility for Michelle and Stan. You can leave if you want and you won't have to feel guilty if you leave. I love our children."

"I love them too—"

"I know you do, but I want—I really want—the responsibility of taking care of them."

I don't remember how that particular discussion went, but a few days later, after learning that the children had been in someone else's care every day the past week, I said, "Charlene, we can't keep living this way."

"I like it this way," she said, "and I like my friends."

I pleaded, argued, yelled, and demanded. Finally I said, "Char, I'll quit my job and leave Savannah, if that's what you want. Anything to get away from this crowd."

"You mean that? That you'd quit your job?"

"I do," I said. "Anything to keep our family together."

"You'd do that for me? Quit your job even?"

"Absolutely," I told her. That seemed to touch her, because in her mind the company took first place in my life.

For the next few months things got better even though we didn't move and I kept my job. We had no more arguments. She still kept hiring baby-sitters and using the nursery all the time. I didn't mind the money she spent, but I wanted her to be with our children and raise them.

Soon she started complaining again about feeling trapped and how much she hated life the way it was. Each time I said, "If you give me custody, you can take off anytime you want."

"You want to get rid of me?" she asked.

"No, but I think you want to be free from us."

"Maybe . . . maybe . . . oh, sometimes I think I do."

"If you give me custody," I said, "you can come and see the children as often as you want. If you just want to come over and hug them on Wednesday night, fine."

"You mean that it would be that simple?" she asked. "And that you would do it that way?"

"I certainly would," I said. I knew that her friends had filled her head with ideas of freedom and getting away from responsibility. I also knew that she felt trapped by life and that at twenty-one she felt she would never have a chance to live in the way her friends indicated was her right to do.

"I'll have to think about it," she said, and that ended the conversation. We never talked about it again.

A month later, we had another severe argument. We argued all along but this was the worst. Those two women had such a hold over Char that they seemed to control her thinking, as though they had programmed her. They convinced her that she was missing out on life. She changed to a different style of clothes that emphasized her figure and, I felt, often made her look cheap and provocative. She got new hairstyles in the latest cuts. Previously she had worn very little makeup, but now she covered her face with it. She didn't even look like the same woman I had married.

One Thursday when I was traveling, I called the house about 9:30 at night. A baby-sitter answered. When I asked to speak to Char, she said, "She asked me to baby-sit at three o'clock this afternoon. I have no idea where she is. She said she'd be back a little later, but I've heard nothing."

I had called from fifty miles away. "Look," I said, "just stay there and I'll get in the car and rush back to Savannah right now."

It was nearly eleven before I got home. The kids were asleep and I asked the baby-sitter to spend the night in the guest room while I went out to look for Charlene. I knew all of her old hangouts and friends and I stayed out almost all night trying to find her. But she was nowhere to be found. She didn't come back the next day, either.

That afternoon one of her friends came to see me. She finally said, "Charlene isn't coming back."

"How do you know that?" I asked her. "Where is she now?"

She said, "Charlene told me she was leaving for California."

"California?" I repeated, hardly able to believe what I had heard.

She had left with a wealthy man whom she had met at the local country club, I later learned. I hadn't even known she ever went there. But then, as I learned in the next few days, there were a lot of things I didn't know about Charlene. The friend who told me about Charlene's leaving also said, "The man told her, 'This is your only chance. Don't even stay long enough to pack a suitcase. Don't wait for anything. Let's just go.' So they left yesterday afternoon."

I shook my head, hardly able to believe it. That's when I realized that I never really knew Charlene.

I had told her she could leave. But I didn't ever believe she would. Despite the growing strain on our marriage and her being still so young, we had mapped out my future. I had been accepted at medical school and was taking courses one night a week as a prerequisite for entering medical training.

Now I knew that I would never be a doctor. I didn't know if I would ever be anything. Charlene had left me. Slowly the reality sank in. She was gone. What kind of man was I? I couldn't even hold a wife. The code of the hills says that a man holds his family together. Although I don't know that anyone actually said it to me, I believed, down deep inside, that no matter how successful a man might be, if he couldn't keep his family straight, he wasn't anything. *I had failed.*

I thought of all those voices in the past. "Knothead." "You damned idiot." "Stupid." Over and over those memories filled my head as I sat there. What made me think I could be a top salesman? What made me think I could do anything? I had put on a good front for a while, but now it had all come out into the open. I was a nothing and everybody else had always known it. Now I knew and it tore me apart.

I was sitting in the living room, hardly able to focus on what was going on around me, when the doorbell rang. Out of my fog I answered. At the door a deputy sheriff handed me a paper. Charlene had filed for a divorce before leaving. She not only wanted a divorce, but the house and custody of our two children.

As soon as he left, tears started to flow. I was upset over everything. But the thought of losing the children was the hardest for me to cope with. I grabbed Michelle and Stan and hugged them. They were far too young to understand what was going on. I hugged and kissed them both. "Daddy's with you. I'm never going to leave you. I'll always be with you, no matter what happens."

9
Dance at Your Own Risk

I was learning a lot about mountains. With some of them I started at the bottom and raced right to the top. There were others where I thought I'd never scale the heights. The deputy sheriff's coming to my door was one of those.

Besides the petition for divorce I read quickly the list of demands. Charlene wanted the house, custody of the children, and large payments. I wadded the papers and threw them on the floor. "What else does she want? In fact, there probably isn't anything else!"

The next day I went to see a lawyer, who heard my statement and read the petition for divorce. He said, "The fact that she left for California means that you've got a good chance."

"How good?" I asked.

He shrugged. "About fifty-fifty."

That didn't seem like much of a chance, but that was 1971 when it was still almost unheard of for a husband to gain custody of his children. I knew right then that I had another mountain to climb.

Well-meaning people came around after that. They told me stories about Charlene, or how badly baby-sitters had treated the children. Maybe they thought they were cheering me up, but they only succeeded in tearing me down more.

One day a neighbor came with even worse news.

"Maybe I shouldn't tell you this," one of Charlene's friends said, "but—"

"You might as well tell me," I said, "it can't be anything worse."

"It might be."

"Tell me anyway," I said, wondering what was coming.

"She's planning to come back for the kids. Just come back and take them," she said.

"Are you sure?"

"She told me," the woman said. "Maybe I shouldn't tell you, but I think she plans to just come back, grab the kids, and take them to California with her."

"She's sure not going to get them! I'll see to that." Inside I was boiling, trying to figure out a plan. It would certainly be easy enough for Char to come back when I was out of town. As their mother, she could take them.

"She loves them, Stan," this friend said. "Despite what she did, Char loves them."

"That may be so," I said, "but she made her choice."

As soon as the woman left, I calmed down a bit, wanting to work out a plan. Almost immediately I knew the answer. I called my folks, told them what had happened, and especially about Charlene's plan to come back.

"So I wondered if I could bring them up there. . . . " Before I had the words out of my mouth, Daddy interrupted: "They're Cottrells and they belong with Cottrells. You bring them up here. I'd like to see anyone come up into these hollows to get those two younguns."

Relieved, I thanked him, but Daddy kept talking.

"They might get into these hollows, but I'll guarantee you, they won't get out. Not with those kids they won't!"

I had hoped Daddy would stand by me. No matter how disappointed he might be in me personally, he lived by the code of the hills. Michelle and Stan were his grandchildren. Blood loyalty came before anything else. Taking them to Kentucky freed me to concentrate on getting over the shock.

When I returned from Kentucky I went back to the house in Savannah. From Charlene's leaving until I returned to that house, I must have operated from a sense of shock and survival. Other than initial anger, during those days I felt no emotion whatever. With cold precision I planned my tactics from engaging a lawyer to taking my children out of state. I even thought, *this isn't so bad after all. I can cope all right.*

Yet when I walked into the empty house, it hit me hard. Charlene was gone. I was alone. I had nobody. The emotions, hidden in the deep freeze, burst forth so strongly I could hardly believe what was happening.

I dropped my suitcase and fell on the floor. Tears came, and had anyone been around, he would have heard some of the loudest bawling and moaning he'd ever heard. I knew what I was doing; I simply couldn't stop myself.

The next three months remain a blur in my memory. Day passed into darkness and back into light again and I had no sense of time. Obviously I didn't remain on the floor for several days, yet I cannot trace a single movement I made.

Depression so enveloped me that only later, when friends told me of their visits, did I realize how bad off I had been. Had anyone ever told me that I would go into a state of severe depression, I would have thought them crazy. Even so, I went through three months of torture.

Bills piled up in the mailbox and I didn't even open them. I didn't have the energy to think about what I owed. Sometime during that period, the power company shut off the electricity. The water company also cut me off. Oddly enough, by some fluke, if I turned on the spiggot, a slight trickle of water came through, enough for me to brush my teeth when I had the energy. I know I must have eaten during those months but that part still remains blurred in my mind.

I remember mostly that I walked around the house crying. Then, tired of crying, I would lie down on the floor and crawl into a fetal position. Never had I been so broken.

Now that I can look back without an emotional fog, I know that my depression involved more than Charlene's leaving me. Our relationship hadn't been good for such a long time, it was almost a relief to have her gone. The depression centered on my whole sense of self-worth. Coming from Kentucky and bred according to the unwritten code of the hills, I tied together manhood and male ego with holding onto a wife.

What kind of man am I? I thought. That question went through my mind hundreds of times. *I can't even hold a wife. I must be useless because no woman wants to live with me.*

I could no longer think of Stan Cottrell who laughed and said, "My security is my ability." Sales, promotions, success, achievements—all these were empty words. From Cottrell the up-and-coming salesman to Cottrell the nobody. From optimism to black pessimism. I didn't run one mile during those three months. I knew I needed to run, but my body wouldn't cooperate. My pain wouldn't let me respond to anything.

One day I finally tried and got half a block from the house. Seeing a neighbor coming toward me, I spun around and raced back to my private prison. I didn't want anyone to see me or talk to me. In my depression, I could only imagine people staring at me and talking about me. I could almost hear people saying things like, "That's the crazy fellow who runs all the time"—and someone answering, "No wonder his wife left him."

One day my manager, Chuck Martin, came to see me. He knocked loudly a dozen times. I didn't answer and he kept knocking.

"Stan, I know you're in there and I'm going to stand out here all day if I have to, and keep knocking until you let me in." Summoning enough energy to walk through the house and to the door, I let him in.

He stared at me for a moment. "You look awful," he said.

I turned around and went back into the living room. I hadn't shaved or showered for days. Anything he said would only confirm my own sense of worthlessness.

"I'm going to lay it on the line, Stan," he said. "By policy, when a man starts going through what you've already gone through, we get rid of him. We know that it takes anywhere from a year to a year and a half for a man to put his life back together again. During that period of time he becomes a liability to us."

I sat there, my head down, unable to look him in the eyes. I knew what was coming next. He was going to terminate me. I didn't care. I didn't feel enough to care about anything.

"Stan," he said, and he laid both his hands on my shoulders and looked at me. "Somehow I know you're going to make it. I'm going to let you walk through this. When you've walked through I think you're going to be okay again and I don't think it's going to be very long."

He didn't terminate me. The words should have encouraged me but they didn't. I was so filled with self-pity, nothing could get through.

After Chuck left, I walked into the bathroom and looked at myself in the mirror. It was the first time I had really thought much about what I looked like in all those weeks. Because of my running I've always maintained a weight of about 135. As I looked at my sunken cheeks, the skin seeming to hang from my arms, I guessed that I weighed 120. I must have looked like someone who'd just come out of a concentration camp.

Knowing how awful I looked didn't motivate me to do anything about it. I simply didn't have the energy. I slumped on the sofa.

How long would this have gone on without the intervention of others? I have no idea. But I do remember how I began to crawl out of my hole and back toward the mountain path again.

A neighborhood couple, Wayne and Betty, came to see me. Charlene and I had known them casually but we had never been close to them. They were simple country folks. Like Chuck, they stayed at the door, knocking, and yelling until I finally let them in.

Wayne made only one statement, "Stan, you're gonna go out with us tonight."

I shook my head, not even having the energy to say no.

Betty said, "Stan, we're not going to take no for an answer. We've been concerned about you and the only way you'll pull out of this is through people like us dragging you out of this house." She laughed, "And, don't forget, he's a little bigger than you."

Wayne was over six feet tall, broad shouldered, with what we called the beer gut.

"You'll never pull out of this as long as you stay cooped up in this house," Betty said. She kept her dark hair dyed a brassy red, had no teeth, and after bearing six children, was badly overweight.

I kept shaking my head. They insisted. Finally it seemed easier to go along with them than to argue. It took less energy to let them half-drag me out of the house than to ignore them.

They drove me to a country music beer joint with the unlikely name of Bowen's Fish Camp. Open only Friday and Saturday nights, they catered to people who liked "real country music."

Not many people would have liked Bowen's Fish Camp. The battered building showed its age. The floor was old and broken, and when people danced I could feel the room shake from twenty feet away. The floor slanted badly and there was no wall at the lower end. If couples got too close to the edge, they slid right into two feet of water—the beginning of the inland waterway. But those country folks didn't seem to notice.

Nobody cared how anyone dressed. Most of them danced barefoot. The men paraded around, barefoot, sometimes bare-chested, but more often wearing only undershirts. Every man looked at least fifty pounds overweight, sporting a beer gut that hung inches over the top of his jeans. The women never wore girdles; their dresses almost split at every seam.

What I liked most about those people was their simple honesty. No pretense of any kind. They worked hard all week and when Friday rolled around, they came to Bowen's Fish Camp to get away from pressures and problems.

As my eyes surveyed the room I saw a sign: Dance at your Own Risk. It struck me as funny and I started to laugh. Then I realized it was the first time I had laughed in almost three months. Something seemed to break inside me and I couldn't stop laughing. Everything was funny. No matter what anyone said, or what music played, I laughed. My neighbors encouraged me and they slurped down one beer after another. I sat there, pushing down cola drinks, not because I liked them, but because I liked beer even less.

A woman, probably ten years older than I, wearing a loose fitting dress that covered up some of her generous lumps, walked over to me and said, "You getting off your rear end, fella? You didn't come here to sit! You gonna dance with me?"

I laughed to hear her talk like that and said, "Well, yeah, I guess I'll dance with you."

"You belong to anyone?"

I shook my head. "No, the last thing I want is to belong to anyone."

She pulled up a chair, sat down, and leaned forward. "Honey, I just want to sit down here and talk to you."

"Sure, ma'am, that's fine. I'd rather talk than dance anyway." Even that struck me funny and I burst out laughing.

We teased back and forth and I was having a good time. Then she leaned closer, "Honey," she said, "some woman sure put a hurtin' on you."

"How do you know that?" I hadn't told her anything about myself.

"Just obvious," she said.

"How? I mean, we've been laughing and carrying on. . . ."

"Honey," she said, and laid her generous-sized arm on mine, "you're a skinny little guy, but I'll tell you this. Whatever woman put a hurtin' on you sure let a good man go."

For at least another ten minutes she edged closer and closer, telling me how much she liked me. Since I had reverted back to laughing at everything, I kidded her about every remark she made.

"How about us seeing each other?" she asked.

I shook my head. "Naw, ma'am."

"Why not? I like you. I like you a lot, honey."

"No use striking a match if you're not going to start a fire," I said, knowing she would understand my statement and not be insulted.

She shrugged her shoulder and yelled across the room for another beer. As she got up, she leaned down and whispered, "I could sure do a lot for you, honey."

She didn't know it, but she had already done a lot for me. I felt as though she had put a Band-Aid on a deep wound. It didn't heal me, but it helped. During those weeks of depression I had groaned and wept over my inadequacy as a man, as a father, as a husband. I blamed my own lack of male sufficiency. Yet, this woman found me interesting and attractive. Her simple words did more for me than she could ever know.

That was the beginning. I wasn't able to run up the mountain, but at least I was beginning to crawl. For six weeks I went back to Bowen's Fish Camp every Friday and Saturday night. My whole life centered around going there. I felt safe with those people; they didn't care who I was, and they never asked. They knew pain in their own lives and they had nothing to hide and nothing to protect. Most of them could hardly speak proper English. They would scratch any part of their anatomy at any time that they wished. Men would come in, grab a swig of beer and the first lady nearby, and start dancing.

One night I left Bowen's Fish Camp knowing I would never be back again. *I didn't need to go back.* Just being with those simple, caring people had started the change in me.

I knew I had to climb mountains again. I began my running routine again. Oddly enough, I hadn't planned to start running; I simply found myself out running again. Because it had been such a long time, it took weeks before I had established my normal level of endurance again. But I was running. Not fast. Not long distances. But running.

10
"For Once I Think You're Doing Something Right"

The depression lifted almost as quickly as it had hit. I rejoined the human race and got down to the business of learning to live once again. Suddenly my heart ached for my two precious children, so I drove to Kentucky and brought them home. My younger sister, Mary, single and twenty-six, came back to Savannah with us and moved in. This was exactly what I had needed. She stayed with us a full year, and I never had to worry about the care of the children when I couldn't be with them.

I still traveled, but I stayed away overnight less frequently. Most weeks, I arranged it so that I had only one night away from home.

When the petition for divorce came due for a hearing, I went to court, along with my sister Mary, and proved to the judge that I could adequately care for my two children and had already established a healthy home life for them. Because Charlene didn't show up, I won full custody.

I no longer had a wife but I had Michelle and Stan and I centered my life around them. "We'll never be separated," I assured them. I determined to be a good father and as much of a mother as I could.

Nine months after the divorce, Charlene countersued, demanding custody of the children. Even though I knew I had a strong case, it was hard on me. Every day I kept asking myself, *What would I do without Michelle and Stan?* I didn't even want to think of an answer.

Char attended the hearing. Over fifty Savannah people came as witnesses on my behalf at the trial and again I won.

I jumped back into the business world with a new enthusiasm, and it paid off. My sales record picked up. A hundred times I wanted to thank Chuck for sticking with me. I determined I wouldn't let him down. He would never regret sticking his neck out for me.

For eighteen of the next twenty-six months I was the top district salesman for our company. I won all kinds of awards, both locally and across the whole industry. I was running more and better than ever; it was now nothing for me to run a hundred miles in a week.

With the flush of selling so easily came the desire for a bigger challenge. I wanted to make up for the lost time after Charlene had left me.

One day I said to Chuck: "I'm a creator, not a curator. The job simply doesn't hold the challenge that it used to." He looked at me, thoroughly surprised. "Most men would cut off both their arms for the sales record you've established," he said.

"I'm not most men," was my reply. I probably sounded boastful. In my immaturity I thought I could do anything in the world I set my mind to. "Look, Chuck, my ability is my security. Just give me a track and I'll run on it and win. I can prove myself at anything I do." Later I would have to eat those words.

"What do you want?" he asked.

"I'd like to be a manager."

"A manager? Come on, Stan. . . . "

"I know the policy of our company. Probably that's a good policy most of the time," I said. The company's policy dictated that a man sell for at least seven years and that after that time he could be considered for a manager's position.

"Look, Chuck," I pleaded, "I have one of the highest call levels in the nation."

"Friend, I know it's high. There ain't no doubt about that."

"High? I have a 9.5. And that's without really knocking myself out."

Chuck knew I had a 9.5 average. He also knew that the average company salesman in America makes an average of 5.4 calls a day, five days a week. But for the next three days he went with me to see for himself. In those three days I made forty-seven quality calls and most of them were for hefty orders or commitments. It absolutely blew his mind. Yet, no matter how many calls I made or how large the orders, company policy was company policy. I could not be considered for promotion until I'd been with the company seven years.

While my selling career started to pick up again, I noticed another trend closer to home. Women started coming to the house. My being the father of motherless children brought out the maternal, and romantic, instincts in women. My children got super treatment from everybody. They had numerous "Aunties" coming around with gifts and offers to baby-sit or take them out so my sister Mary could have free time. They constantly wanted to feed the children. I remember telling Mary, "You pet the calf to get the cow." Those women, for all their kindness toward my children, made it clear that they wouldn't turn down a date if I ever asked.

For a long time I couldn't respond to any woman. I was ashamed and embarrassed that I was a "grass widower." Although I had gotten past the depression, I couldn't face the prospect of involvement with a woman again. Strangely enough, the more I pulled back, the more attractive certain women pictured me. Finally, I dated simply because I wanted the companionship of an adult female.

I had one unfortunate experience. A lovely blond started coming to the house, bringing gifts and playing with the children. I probably grew more serious about her than any of the others I dated. Then, one evening, we were sitting on my back porch. It was a quiet, warm evening; we sat close and I put my arm around her. She snuggled closer and our words got more and more serious. She laid her head on my shoulder and began stroking the back of my head. I leaned forward to kiss her, but just then young Stan, two years old, came to the door.

"Daddy," he called, "can I have some juice?"

Before I could say anything, the woman sat up straight and said, "Why don't you tell that little brat to get out of here?"

"Just a minute," I told Stan, "and Daddy will take care of you." I jumped up, grabbed the woman's arm and half pulled her off the porch.

"What's going on?" she screamed.

"You get out of here!"

The startled look in her eyes told me she still had not comprehended what had happened.

"I'm a man," I said, "and I try to be a gentleman. But let me tell you something: I don't ever want to see you again. Because, if I do, I'm liable to forget I'm a gentleman and bust you right upside of your head with my fist."

"Stan! Have you gone crazy? What's. . . . "

"Nobody talks about my kids that way! Nobody calls my kids brats!"

I got her all the way to the car, pulled the door open, pushed her inside, and kicked the car. "Don't you ever show your face around here again!" I said.

Of course I had overreacted. But several things were going on inside me. I was building a new life for myself, a life centered around my children. I didn't want them to have any more pain. For at least a year I went to bed with the two of them sleeping on either side of me. I needed their closeness but I also wanted them to know how much I loved them. In my own way, I tried to be everything they needed—father, mother, friend, guardian, even playmate. They came to me with their problems, and joys, and needs, the way most children go to their mother. I became overprotective and probably spoiled them, but I wanted to erase the pain in their lives and replace it with love.

During that first year, however, I didn't know how to talk to the children about Charlene. Three-year-old Michelle would go to bed with me and almost every night she'd say, "I don't think my mommy's coming home tonight."

I couldn't answer her, other than to say, "Not tonight, sweetheart." Many of those nights I turned my head away so that she wouldn't see the tears in my eyes.

During those days, Michelle had one expression she used with almost every sentence she spoke. "But my daddy. . . . " I became her authority for everything and she focused her life on me as I had already done on her and young Stan. She was too young to understand words like *divorce* and *custody.* I thought it wiser not to say anything. I answered her questions in simple one- and two-word sentences. Even at three, she understood more than I gave her credit for.

One afternoon, I came home early. I was sitting on the sofa, reading the paper and she was looking out the living room window. She stayed there for an especially long time. "My mommy is never coming back," she said. It wasn't a question. She somehow had reasoned it out. From that time on, Michelle never asked about her mother returning.

I had one special friend during that time, Joe, a pharmacist in Savannah. Joe will never know how much he helped me climb back up the mountain. He did and said outrageous things to keep conversation light and enjoyable. I often called him "Crazy Man" because of his wild sense of humor. No matter how low I felt when we got together, just being with him gave me a tremendous boost.

One day we drove eighty miles to Brunswick, on the Georgia coast, so that we could see a live oak tree Joe had climbed when a kid. Crazy? Of course, but very good therapy for me. But something better than therapy came out of that ride. Joe introduced me to an old friend of his, and she had a roommate named Carol Odum.

When we met, I must have stared at her. I remember thinking, *this is the most beautiful girl I've seen in a long, long time.* Her dark hair, olive complexion, and indescribable blue-green eyes fascinated me. When time came for Joe and me to leave, I determined to see Carol again.

As much as I wanted to see her, I still hesitated. I had already struck out at marriage and I was afraid to go up to bat again. But two weeks later, I found an excuse to visit Brunswick. I looked up Carol's number and called.

"Just passing through," I said, "and, well, I was wondering if I could drop by and see you?"

"Yes, that would be all right," she said.

I felt awkward, hardly knowing what to say. I had dated a lot of women in the previous weeks, but no one like Carol. With most of the others, I didn't care whether I saw them again or not. Because Carol was so different, I didn't want to mess it up, and that scared me. And being scared, I felt ill at ease.

We spent about an hour together, then made a date for a week later when I would come through again. A second date followed, and a third. I wanted this relationship to be right. I went out with Carol six times before I ever kissed her.

After eight or nine dates, I called my mother. "Momma," I said, "I'm ashamed of a lot of things I've done in the past. I've really been down during this last year and my life's been a mess. But things are going to get better for a change. Being with Carol makes me know that."

Momma, not having met Carol, sensed that this one was different from any of the others. "I'm happy for you, Stanley junior," she said.

One day I asked Carol to go to Florida with me. "I want you to meet the Boatwrights. They're great people." They lived less than two hours' drive from Brunswick.

"They're great people," I said, "and we can swim or do anything else you like."

"Stan, I don't go in for that kind of thing."

Then it hit me what she meant. I intended only to take her to meet my special friends as one further step toward letting her into my life.

"Carol, my two children will be with us. All I want you to do is go with me, meet my friends. If you don't like them, we will hop in the car and head right back here to your apartment."

She agreed to go and the four of us drove to Orange Park. By then, I had already fallen in love with Carol. In wanting the Boatwrights to meet her, I really wanted their approval. They had been like parents to me and so caring. It became important to me that they meet and like Carol.

They liked Carol immediately. They loved me enough that they probably would have accepted anyone I brought there. But it went deeper. They genuinely liked her. And Carol liked them.

The day came when I knew I had to let Carol know how deeply I felt. Yet, because of my failed marriage, I hardly knew how to approach her. I knew I had been waiting all my life to meet Carol and I wanted to marry her.

My mother called her parents and invited Carol to spend the weekend in our home. We did it properly so that Carol never had to worry about anything wrong taking place. She was twenty-three and had high moral standards. It was so refreshing to meet someone like her. Many young couples I knew never bothered or worried about parental consent. But I wanted this relationship to be right from the very start.

Both my parents made Carol feel right at home. And she liked them immediately. As was his custom, my father sat in the yard after supper, chewing tobacco and whittling. Carol went outside to sit beside Daddy and to enjoy the country air.

"Would you like a chaw of tobacco?" Daddy asked her.

His offer took Carol by surprise. For a moment she hesitated; never in her life had she wanted to taste chewing tobacco. But she did want Daddy to like her.

"Why sure," she said, and accepted a chaw. The first taste was "indescribable," but she persisted. The plug Daddy gave her wasn't big at all, but it was strong—Warren County Twist. It almost made her sick. Yet, she was determined that Daddy was going to like her. And like her he did.

The following day Daddy and I were working in the barn and he looked at me and said, "Son, for once in your life, I think you're doing something right." Then he walked away. That was his way of saying he approved of Carol.

While I appreciated his approval, I didn't need it. I knew that I loved Carol and eventually wanted to marry her. We began spending more time together. I burned up the road between Savannah and Brunswick, getting there as often as I could.

One evening we walked along the beach together. I can't recall ever seeing such a beautiful tropical evening. Everything looked like a love scene out of a Hollywood film, from the quiet lapping of the waves to the sun slowly sinking behind the horizon. As it grew dark, the stars filled the sky and I couldn't see a single cloud. We walked along, holding hands, and I felt such a deep sense of peace.

I had been wearing a jacket and Carol's hand felt cold. "You chilly?" I asked.

"A little."

I took my jacket off and wrapped it around her shoulders. I left my arm there. We stopped and she turned slightly, facing me. I kissed her gently and didn't want to let go.

"Carol, it's hard for me to think about spending the rest of my life without you."

"What's that supposed to mean?"

A state of shock came over me and I didn't know what to say next. I loved her and had no doubts about my feelings, but I feared she would reject me.

"Well, uh . . . " I said.

"Are you asking me to marry you, Stan?"

"Absolutely."

"I can't imagine my going through life without you either," she said.

Her words were the sweetest music I had ever heard. She had that same deep love for me that I had for her.

Still, during the next weeks, I would get on a self-pity jag every once in a while. Charlene had taken a big bite out of me. Though Carol had done much to help me heal, I had battles with self-doubt and depression. Being a grass widower, I wondered if I were doing the right thing or if I were just going to mess up Carol's life.

One day she said to me, "I've listened to your whining about Charlene long enough. When are you going to stop whimpering?" I hadn't been aware of how much crying I had done and how much self-pity there had been. Her words shocked me.

"Stan, I love you," she said. "I accept you and I accept your children. I know that in marrying you I'm getting a package deal and that's all right with me. But I'm not marrying Charlene and I'm not going to marry her shadow. I know everything that I need or ever want to know about Charlene and about your past."

I needed to hear those words. I also knew that the final scars had healed. Carol loved me and she wanted me to put my past failures behind me. Her straightforward courage enabled me to do just that.

From that moment, I determined not to resurrect the memories of life with Char. And since that time, I've not needed to.

We planned an August 1972 wedding and everything went beautifully. A few weeks before the wedding Carol's mother called me aside.

"Stan, Carol's a Christian," she said, "and I raised her to be a Christian."

"Yes, ma'am," I said, wondering what was coming next.

"Do you believe the children should be raised in a Christian home?"

"Yes, ma'am," I said.

"What role does Christ have in your life?"

Naturally I didn't like the question and I felt uncomfortable. I didn't want to offend Carol's mother for anything. So I decided to bluff my way through. After all, I was a good salesman. Besides, I had been around the church enough as a boy to know the language of religious people. I knew the answer she wanted.

"Ma'am, I want you to know that my Momma raised me according to the gospel and Christian ways."

I added some other things, not intentionally lying to her, but not giving away anything either. I gave answers, being careful not to invite her to ask me anything else. Apparently this satisfied Carol's mother and we didn't talk about religion again.

"We want you and Carol to be happy and will always stand behind you," she said.

During our courtship, the children called her Carol. Carol suggested this. "I don't want to take their mother's place. I'm not their natural mother, but I'll love them as much as if I were."

And she did. Both children responded to her, and while they didn't understand all the implications of marriage, they did understand that when Carol and I married, she would live with us.

Immediately after the wedding, Carol and I planned to go away for a few days. I held Michelle and Stan and told them how much I loved them and how much I would miss them.

Michelle looked at me and said, "Daddy, I 'cided something. Me and Stan."

"What's that, sweetheart?"

"We're going to call her *Mommy* now and not Carol."

"I think that's a good idea," I said, deeply touched and grateful that I didn't have to suggest it.

"That all right, Daddy?"

"It's perfect," I said and hugged her again.

They went to Carol and called her Mommy. From that time on, they have called her nothing else.

My life had turned around. Not only meeting and marrying Carol. Not only watching her become a wonderful mother to the children. But even my career took on a new direction. Within a week after our wedding I received an offer for a new job. I took that job, becoming an assistant director of allied health education in a Savannah medical center. The opportunity made me ecstatic.

"Carol, I feel as though I've been given a second chance in life."

"Oh, Stan, God is so good to us, isn't He?"

I didn't answer, but I thought, *what's God got to do with this anyway? I've worked hard. I've earned the opportunity.*

I had a lot of surprises in store for me.

11
A Missed Plane—A Second Chance?

Running played an important role in my being offered the new job at the Savannah hospital. Several doctors recommended me when the position came open. They wrote lengthy recommendations stating that my professionalism impressed them and remarking on my background in health and physical education. Several of them mentioned my weekly runs, which by then were totalling 120 miles.

The new job not only meant a good salary and no travel, it meant teaching. I had loved teaching in high school and this opportunity presented me with a new challenge. I taught in the core curriculum in five allied health fields. This included students in programs such as LPN (Licensed Practical Nurse), respiratory therapy, and EMT (Emergency Medical Technician). I taught anatomy, biology, and microbiology—and even math, which was a shock to me. In teaching that subject, I learned math for the first time and stayed about one hour ahead of my students.

While with the hospital I don't think a single week passed without some company trying to hire me for a sales job. Finally, one firm made me such an attractive offer that I couldn't refuse. It was a German pharmaceutical company just getting started in America. I saw it as a chance to get in on the ground floor. In six months I had been given responsibility for half of the state of Georgia, a territory previously covered by five salesmen. I personally sold enough so that company sales increased 205 percent over the previous year's total by all five men.

I didn't accomplish this through my sales activities alone. Falling back on my experience with Squibb and my reputation with many doctors, I made myself available to hospitals for in-service programs. Other salesmen simply sold; I decided to work smarter rather than harder.

At the end of six months—in August 1974—the company asked me to step into the position of product manager. It was a dream job, but it meant moving to Connecticut. I loved Savannah and hated the thought of leaving it. So did Carol.

For one thing, we had bought our first home. And in June, Carol had given birth to our daughter, Jennifer, a sweet, blue-eyed blond. It was not an easy time to think of relocating.

Yet, the real reason I hesitated at the new job offer was that it scared me. I had come a long way since my Kentucky days of outhouses and no running water, and I had just enough insecurity to question my ability. I wondered, could I keep doing as well? Was I really a good salesman, or had it been some kind of freakish luck? Most of the time I bounded with enthusiasm, and with that enthusiasm, a conceited kind of assurance. But once in a while, doubts set in. Would I fail, like Uncle Roy had done?

Those negative voices from childhood still taunted me, but not very much. Every success enabled me to thumb my nose at them all. I called Daddy and Momma a lot, every time I accomplished anything of importance. Momma did most of the talking, but I knew my father was listening. He never said much but I hoped he was proud of me.

While I hesitated about moving, I also knew how large companies operate. To refuse a promotion boxes a person in. I wanted to move upward. Everything in my nature propelled me toward advancing my career. So, I accepted the promotion.

In August I began commuting in and out of Savannah. Sunday afternoons would find me on a flight bound for New York. I would return home every Friday night. This was the way we lived for five months. Carol was virtually a widow during those months, and she surely had her hands full with baby Jennifer, and with Michelle and Stan III, who were 6 and 4. Finally, in December 1974, our house in Savannah sold and we moved to Bethel, Connecticut.

For the next eighteen months life offered me one great challenge after another. Under the leadership of Tony Zinnanti, a manager's manager, opportunity after opportunity opened up for me to deal with prestigious advertising agencies, develop new programs, launch and teach seminars, make educational films, and do business with some of the top leaders in the medical world.

However, Carol didn't find the new situation rewarding at all. She's a sociable person by nature, but she simply could not make friends. As far as I know, she cried every day during those eighteen months. When the opportunity came for me to become a regional sales representative in Atlanta, she was greatly relieved.

The day we moved into our home on the north side of Atlanta, the entire neighborhood turned out to meet us. At least it seemed that way. People came by to welcome us, bringing coffee and fresh-baked pies and cookies. It was great to be back "home."

After a year, I moved from regional sales manager to become the director of national marketing. It was the greatest challenge of my career. But four weeks later, the job was taken away from me. Our growing company had made a number of significant acquisitions of smaller companies and one condition of the agreement was that the man whose company we purchased would be the director of marketing.

I felt cheated, and yet that's the way corporate life works. I took this as a personal defeat. I had been a company man who had proven his loyalty, and instead of being rewarded, I got pushed back.

A few days later the president called me in. "If you'll stay with us and go along with this," he said, "you'll be rewarded." I found out later that the company was getting ready to go international and they were grooming me to become the international director of marketing. "Just go back for a few days to your old job and do what you did before," the president asked.

Groaning inside, I did as he asked. And because I've always liked the challenge of selling, I went back with a high incentive. I wanted to prove to them that I could achieve, in case they had any doubts. Results came in and sales boomed.

Yet, despite the success, I didn't like myself very well. I had begun to slip away from the basic principles my parents had bred in me—the code of the hills, honesty, and keeping my word. I had started to use people for my own advantage. The things I did, while not illegal, bothered me, and inside I knew they were wrong.

Everybody else does it, I would tell myself; that's the way to get ahead in business. I salved my troubled conscience by vaguely committing myself to change once I made it to the top. Foolish reasoning, of course, but in those days I wanted only to reach the top of the mountain. I didn't particularly care how I got there. Things might never have changed for me except that one day I had a ten-minute delay.

It happened in Jasper, Alabama, in April 1978, where I met with a hospital administrator. After our meeting I planned to leave on a plane for Winston-Salem, North Carolina, but the administrator urged me to stay for lunch, hinting at the possibility of additional business contacts. We continued talking business over lunch and when I looked at my watch I realized that it was almost time for my flight. Since most planes don't leave exactly on time, I felt I had a fair chance of making the flight. We tried. At the Huntsville airport I waved goodbye and rushed inside to the ticket counter.

"Sorry," the clerk said, "you missed your plane by exactly ten minutes."

I shrugged, walked over to the counter of a different airline and after an hour's wait, left Huntsville.

The incident would have ended there except that when I got to my hotel room in Winston-Salem very late that night and turned on the television, I learned that the plane I had missed by ten minutes had crashed over New Hope, Georgia. Everyone on board, including the crew, was killed.

Hearing the news sent me into a daze. *Ten minutes,* I kept thinking. *By ten minutes' delay my life has been spared.*

One question came to my mind. Why? Why had I been given a second chance? I couldn't think of a single answer. I didn't like myself, as a result of the way I had been living. I guess I felt that I didn't deserve a second chance. Yet I could not simply dismiss it as fate or just one of those inexplicable things in life.

The next morning when I wakened, I was very glad to be alive. The colors in the trees and the hills of Winston-Salem never looked so vivid. When I stood to speak before an audience at the hospital later that morning I said: "I'm glad to be here today." And I really meant that.

12
Four Hundred Five Miles? Impossible!

I remained loyal to the company, but to say that I wasn't entirely satisfied would be an understatement. I was frustrated with the ups and downs of corporate life. But I couldn't make a decent living teaching. I was doing a lot of soul searching, asking myself: What can I do? What do I want to do? What kind of job satisfies and supports me?

Running provided the missing dimension during those days. I had been competing in 10k (6.2 miles) events. I didn't win many, because my thing is endurance, not speed. I can go on forever. I managed to stay up with the top competition, and I also helped organize local runs in and around Atlanta.

As I began to identify myself, in my own mind at least, as an athlete interested in fitness I realized that I needed something to make me stand out so that people would listen to what I have to say. I needed something to give me credentials. The idea of corporate fitness was just taking shape in my thinking.

About that time I read about a group of seven men who had planned a ten-day run across Georgia, intending to average forty miles a day. Two of them dropped out after the second day. On the third day it was quits for all.

I kept thinking about that. I had once run fifty-five miles in one day, I reminded myself. And I didn't know much about running then.

I could beat their records. For a while I tried to forget the idea, but it kept coming back. Why couldn't I run completely across the state of Georgia? Four hundred and five miles. I could do that. I was running at least twenty miles a day at that time and I figured, with proper planning, I could average forty miles a day and "run Georgia."

The work with the company became more depressing and for the first time in my life, I gave less than 100 percent to the job. I had always worked so hard that the company usually got double duty out of me. But for a three-month period, I didn't put that kind of effort into my job. Instead of starting my job at 6:00 A.M. I went out to run. I would spend four hours just running. For the next twelve weeks I spent almost every morning out on the roads, burning up my shoes, and chalking up the miles. During those weeks I kept track and my lowest week was 196 miles; most weeks I finished a little over 200.

Just to run a long distance such as across Georgia wasn't enough. I had to decide how to set up the run, how to publicize it, how to get it sponsored. I knew of and had helped a number of charitable organizations get behind everything from walk-athons to rock-athons to 10k races.

I approached several groups. "I'll run for you," I said. "You sponsor the race, take care of the publicity, and any money you can raise you keep." I was sure they'd grab the idea. But the groups didn't grab the idea. They told me that such an idea was crazy (in words less strong than that). They constantly received crackpot ideas for fund-raising.

Finally I contacted the Georgia chapter of the American Lung Association. I said, "It'll be a good way for you to kick off your Christmas seal program and get a lot of free publicity."

They talked to me a long time—more than any of the other groups. "We'll get back to you," came as their final statement. At least they hadn't totally rejected the idea.

A few days later they called back. "If you can get a corporation to put up $1,000, we'll go along with it and handle all the publicity."

"I'll be back in touch," I said. I knew I could get the thousand, but had the feeling that they didn't. It's an interesting phenomenon in sponsorship as I was to learn later when I worked on my Run For

America. If you can get the first sponsor, you can usually get others. Most companies ask, almost from the start, "Who else is sponsoring?" If you can tell them of at least one, they'll give more serious consideration.

While not sure, I suspected that the executive played that same game with me. If I was some crackpot I wouldn't be back in touch with them and they'd have no problem. But if one corporation agreed, then they'd see it as legitimate.

Immediately I called a friend, Jim Hansford, an executive with the American Fitness Center, and explained my idea.

"Sounds like a great idea," he said.

That was the kind of talk I wanted to hear.

"I'd like the American Fitness Center to be tied in with your run and the Lung Association. We'll do it."

What pride it gave me to call the Lung Association back, less than an hour later. When the executive got on the phone and I identified myself, I blurted out, "You got your thousand dollars!"

True to their promise, the American Lung Association got behind me and did a splendid job of promoting the run. Every paper in the state, it seemed, called me for interviews. I had a constant parade of radio and TV people coming to me. Most of them looked upon it as a bizarre kind of thing, but it was news.

"I'm going to run this in seven days," I told interviewers. "I'll start at Chattanooga, Tennessee, right on the Georgia line, and seven days later I'll meet you at the Florida state line."

After that the phone calls and letters came, many from doctors. "Stan, we're concerned for your health," they would say. "Don't do this to yourself."

Well-meaning friends even called their doctors who, in turn, called me. "You'll ruin your body," one doctor said. He came to my home with a stack of drawings and diagrams. "It's physically impossible for the human body to endure that kind of relentless torture. Even if you make the run, you'll probably never walk again."

He said it seriously and meant it.

I thanked him and said, "Maybe so, but I'm going to do it anyway."

Those folks who tried to stop me only reinforced my decision. It was the old thing again. As soon as someone told me I didn't have any sense, or that I couldn't do something, it only made me more determined than ever.

By the time the run actually began, I had been in constant training for twelve weeks. Most people didn't know that I was already covering half the distance weekly.

A few days before the run, a lovely woman from the Lung Association called me aside. "Stan, whatever you do, at least try to make it to Atlanta." Atlanta was approximately 120 miles.

"You don't think I'll make it?" I asked. "You don't think I'll make the whole 405 miles?"

"I always believe in a back-up plan," she said. "If you can just make it to Atlanta, it'll be all right." She held a sheet of paper in her hand for me to see: "A press release explaining," she said, "explaining why you had to stop the run."

"Ma'am, you can just throw that paper away right now."

"One hundred twenty miles is a long run," she said, "a very long run. I don't know anyone who can go that far."

"It may be a good run and a long run, but just to Atlanta isn't 405 miles."

We talked a while and finally I said, "I just want one thing from you, ma'am."

"Of course, just—"

"When I reach that finish line, I want to look up and see you standing there, shredding that press release into thousands of pieces."

She smiled. "You complete the run and I'll be there. Promise."

She didn't know it, but she had just given me the biggest impetus of all. I would prove to her and to everyone else in the world that I could make that run. If I had harbored doubts before, they were gone now. I would complete that race if I had to crawl the last twenty miles.

On October 31, 1978, I started, at 5:00 A.M. on a very cool Saturday, from Chattanooga. The American Lung Association had coordinated everything well. They had lined up activities in almost every small town along the route. Mayors came out and greeted me. I would make a brief speech about fitness and health. City council members thrust proclamations into my hands, calling it everything from Georgia Fitness Day to Georgia Lung Association Week. School children lined the roads, holding up banners. Twice that first day I stopped, gathered the children around me and urged them to take care of their greatest natural resource, their bodies. Interviewers tagged along. A few of them came out and ran a mile or two with me.

The Lung Association provided people along the route. Tommy, a neighbor of mine in Tucker, drove a van—carrying my personal gear—and watched over me like a mother hen.

I ran seventy miles that first day. The next morning my stiffened body rebelled against movement but I pushed myself on. "You're going to do it," I said over and over. And somehow I got out there on the road and started out Sunday morning, determined to make Atlanta before dark.

Just north of Cartersville, Georgia, a man with a CB radio pulled up beside me. "You're the runner? You're the runner?" he asked. He was so excited, he could only keep repeating the same question.

I kept running along and said, "Sure am."

He pulled his CB mike to his mouth. "Hey, folks, I got him here! I'm driving right next to him. That runner!"

He thrust the mike at me. "Say something!"

"Hello!" I said and before I could add another word he had the mike again. "See, folks, that's the runner. He's here! Really here and I've just been talking to him!"

He waved, thanked me again, and drove off.

A little later I reached one town where I had to wait for twenty minutes because the mayor had overslept. I spent the time shaking hands, answering questions, and laughing with people. Instead of wearing me out, just being around all those people stirred me up.

That afternoon as I neared Atlanta, something happened to me. I fell in love with long-distance running. I had always liked running and it had been such a vital part of my life. But this was different. I knew I was happier hitting the pavement, despite the pain and physical agony, than doing anything else I had ever done. My body kept trying to get me to stop, but my mind said, "We're going to the Florida line!"

I learned then that a lot of strange things happen on long runs. The humorous and the frightening both take place, but it always keeps running from becoming dull for me.

Just before reaching Barnesville (south of Atlanta), I saw a car coming toward me. On the passenger's side a man was stretched well out the window. From the distance I thought he was some overexuberant fan who wanted to shake my hand. As the car drew closer, I saw that he was swinging a golf club widely and screaming at the top of his lungs, "I'll kill you! I'll kill you!" He punctuated his words with wilder swings. The car kept coming closer and I left the road and dashed into a yard just to get away.

Having no idea what that was all about, I headed back to the road and resumed running. The Lung Association people had roared on ahead to Barnesville to make sure everything was ready for my arrival. My own follow-up van, for some reason, had slowed down and was trailing at least half a mile behind me.

I kept running and happened to turn my head. Then I heard a shouting voice again. The same man in the same car. He was screaming even louder and swinging more wildly and mouthing every word of profanity he knew. Again, I ran off the road and out of his way.

Tommy saw it this time and pulled up close behind me, so I didn't worry about the man anymore. I went on into Barnesville and would have forgotten the incident, except that the man appeared a third time.

On the south side of town his car pulled up and the man thrust a handful of bills at me. "Hey, I'm sorry, fella," he said. "Honest."

"I don't want your money," I said and kept on running.

In embarrassed tones he told me that he had fallen madly in love with a woman and she had been seeing another man. He didn't know the man's name, only that he did a lot of running. In those days, running had not become a big thing in small Georgia towns. "So when I saw you on the road, I—well, I sorta guessed—"

"Just take your money and get out of here!" I yelled. "I don't want it and I'll tell you something else, you could have killed me!"

He apologized again and roared away.

By the time he was out of sight, the humor of the situation hit me and I laughed and laughed.

Two hours later I met the meanest dog I've ever encountered. He came running out of a man's yard and stopped in front of me. He bared his teeth and growled, ready to attack. I've learned that normally I can yell something like "Sam!" with authority and a dog takes off. But this one stayed his ground. I stopped, and looked at the animal, not sure of my next move.

Just then I heard a shotgun and as I turned I saw a man shooting into the air and running toward us. "Git going, you crazy dog!" he yelled, and fired again. I've seldom seen a dog move as fast as that one did.

The farmer smiled then, waved at me, and said, "Sorry for the inconvenience." Greatly relieved and somewhat amused, I ran on.

Near the town of Vienna, a woman pulled up beside me. She wore her hair filled with rollers, and a cigarette dangled from her mouth. "If you want some good exercise," she said, "you can help me unload this." She nodded her head and I saw that the back of her pickup was loaded with plastic bags of garbage. About two tenths of a mile ahead I saw a large dumpster. She pulled on ahead.

When I reached the dumpster, I jumped on the pickup and started tossing the garbage bags into the dumpster. Then, finishing up, I jumped back down and dashed down the road. The woman never said a word; she just watched me work. Afterward Tommy said, "I'll bet she's asking, 'Who was that masked man?' "

At the end of the fifth day I reached Valdosta. I had run 382 miles. I could have gone on then to the Florida line, but the Lung Association people asked me to wait until the next morning.

"You've already set some record," one of their members said. "If you'll finish in the morning we can get much wider publicity."

The next morning Jim Hansford from the American Fitness Center joined me, along with a dozen other runners. Jim had never run twenty miles in his life, but he did the whole twenty-three that day.

As we hit the Florida line, flashbulbs popped and reporters surrounded me, asking dozens of questions.

When they finally started to move away, I saw the young woman from the Lung Association. She held up the prepared press release and with a wide smile, she tore it into pieces. "You have to understand," she said, "we wanted to be prepared for the unexpected. Really, we're proud of you."

I laughed because I understood. But I could say only one thing to her. "My dear, I'd already visualized your tearing that paper up a thousand times." Then I explained that thinking about her destroying the paper had been one of my biggest motivators.

"If anyone wants me to try harder, all he has to say is, 'Stan, you're crazy. You can't do it.' "

I tried to remain calm as the woman walked away, but inside I was euphoric. I thought: *I'm well on my way to becoming a whole person. I can do something. I can run long distances. This is the first one. Wait till Daddy hears about this!*

13
I Launch My Ship and It Sinks

Success had smiled on me. The path led always upward and "full success," or so it seemed, was always yet one step further. My 405-mile run told the world that I was a true ultramarathon runner. Life kept getting better for me. I had only one serious problem: I still didn't like myself very much.

More than once I looked at myself in the mirror and winced. I had gotten ahead in the corporate world, but had I paid too high a price?

For several months I went through a stage where I constantly searched myself and wondered what I was doing with my life, where I really wanted to go, what I wanted my life to count for. The flaming plane crash frequently came to mind. If God had actually given me another chance in life, what was I doing with that chance?

I couldn't even answer that question. I knew that life ought to be more than I had and yet I didn't know what that "more" was.

The enthusiasm I had experienced in the world of sales and promotion left me. I hated many of the things I said and did to gain business. I had played the phoney by saying things I didn't mean. Even though I got results, I didn't always like my actions.

For instance, being lulled by my drive for success, I befriended people until I got them signed as steady customers. Then I dropped them and moved on to new prospects. Cultivating true friendships would block my time and energy from reaching new people. Success in business meant constantly widening my circle of people.

I grew tired of the tactics, unhappy with myself, bored with making the same sales pitch time after time. I needed a newer and higher mountain.

In my travels, I had come across countless executives caught up in running the business race who had gained their wealth but lost their health in the pursuit. Again the idea of corporate fitness surged to the forefront in my thinking. People can have both—business success and physical fitness—I thought.

All over America, fifty-year-old men have invested themselves emotionally and psychologically in their businesses, to the exclusion of almost everything else. By middle life, their bodies have paid the price with heart attacks, ulcers, and cirrhosis of the liver. They kill themselves by heavy smoking, heavy stress, and no physical exercise.

Bing! *Corporate fitness.* That's the need, I told myself. I knew the next step was to set up a fitness concept and then promote it.

Excited by the possibilities, I created a whole approach to corporate fitness for the company I worked for. I planned for a new division within the company, which I would head up. I knew, for instance, that if employers gave their workers incentives to go two blocks away and get into shape, few would take advantage of it. But if we brought the experts to the offices and factories, it would succeed.

When presenting my proposal to the leadership in our company, I got more enthusiastic about corporate fitness than I had about anything in a long time. "We'll bring doctors right to the offices. We'll have stress tests right at the place of business. Have brown-bag seminars. . . ."

"Stan, you're a visionary," one executive said. The others agreed with him.

Actually, I had only one problem: I was five years ahead of time. Five years later corporate fitness became the *in* thing.

During those days of planning and dreaming, I kept running. As I sped down those roads alone, my best ideas came to me. I envisioned a nation of healthy men and women less dependent upon medical treatment because they had learned to prevent many illnesses.

Not only did I enjoy my daily runs, but I started running longer distances, thirty or forty miles. The company, rather than frowning on the idea of my long runs, encouraged me. When I finished the 405-mile run across Georgia, interviewers came from everywhere. And they always asked me: "What kind of work do you do?" I would mention the name of my company. It was free advertising. Beyond that, the spotlight on my running showed people that I was an expert in physical fitness.

Unfortunately, my company was not impressed. They quite diplomatically rejected the total package because they didn't think it would work. For a while I didn't know what to do next. It seemed that I wouldn't be happy remaining with the company. I wanted to forge ahead with new dreams, but they didn't want to participate in those dreams.

It all came to a head one day when I had a long talk with myself. I was thirty-four years old. A college graduate—which was pretty good, coming from the hollows of Kentucky. (A friend, Bully Webb, called me "the Cub Run holler scholar!") I was an outstanding salesman. I'd had experience teaching seminars and workshops, had been product manager, and had dealt with all kinds of people, working under constant stress. I had sold both tangible and intangible products.

When I asked myself what I wanted to do with the rest of my life, I knew what it was: I'd like to start my own company, teaching health and fitness. And in addition to getting people into shape, I had another concept—Wellness-Illness. I envisioned hospitals as centers for teaching people how to stay well and how to cope with illness. I had that idea early in 1978.

As I was to discover, I was again several years too early. But I didn't know that. I felt I was ready to take the plunge. So, early in 1978 I quit my job and launced my ship. I hired a lawyer and incorporated Life Dynamics, a company whose purpose would be to do the things I envisioned. I *knew* that it would succeed and never had a doubt in my mind. I had made a success of anything I had tried to sell. Why shouldn't this be the same, or even greater?

Through friends, I made contacts and put together a stock package. I didn't know anything about stocks—only what the man told me who helped me set it up. That was my first mistake. He was out of touch with the investor market, but I didn't know it then.

As the chief salesman, I went out to contact investors. Former customers and coworkers had encouraged me when I talked of my plans, but when I actually put the plan into action, they either lost interest or implied that they were in no position to invest.

I had enough savings put back to last three months. Surely by then, I told everyone, the company would be solid. After all, I could sell anything. In those next three months, I made hundreds of calls. People smiled a lot, warmly shook my hand, and welcomed me, but I never sold the first dollar's worth of stock.

In the meantime I did some dumb things. I was so cocksure of success that I rented office space and hired three staff people. They were all talented, but none were especially talented in sales. I watched my bank account dwindle. Each day my dream dissolved just a little more.

Then, at almost the last minute, a multi-millionaire to whom I had sent a stock proposal through a friend, called me.

"He would like you to come to Nashville and meet him," his secretary said. We set up the date. A ticket was waiting for me at the Atlanta airport. Surely, this was the miracle I had waited for, I thought. Simply his sending me a round-trip, first-class ticket indicated his eagerness to invest in my corporation.

At the Nashville airport the man met me, a bottle of rum in one hand and a cigar in the other. He greeted me warmly. He drank his rum straight and it amazed me to see the amount this mammoth-sized fellow drank. Large, fleshy, and foul-mouthed, he seemed like anything but a millionaire. We passed from the airport and got into his Cadillac, and all the time he carried on a monologue, telling me about Nashville.

Once inside the Cadillac, he sat silently for a moment and then said, "Son, I'm going to tell you something. You're crazier than an outhouse rat if you think you're coming up here and I'm writing you a check for an investment."

I must have stared because I didn't know what to say.

"I don't know you from the wind blowing," he said.

I felt like saying, "Just take me back to the airport. You've insulted me and had your fun."

"You're not a businessman, are you?" he asked.

"Why, yessir I am—I've been in the business world for ten years."

"No!" he thundered, peppering his phrases with profanity, "I mean a *business*man. You're not a businessman. How many businesses you started before?"

"Uh, none," I said.

"I know. I know," he waved his hand, silencing me from trying to defend myself. "You've been a salesman and you've done a lot of things. But until you've started your own business, you're not a businessman."

"Put that way, I guess not."

"And I don't know who dreamed up this stock package for you but I'd have to be on dope to buy the prospectus you have. This is just an antiquated piece of slop.

"To begin with," he said, "the stock you're offering are preferred, they're nonpre-emptive, nonvoting, and there's no par value."

I wanted to stop him and tell him that one of his best friends, an executive in his own company, had set it up for me. Instead I listened.

For a full hour he lectured me, giving me a short course in investments. I cowered, and felt angry, but at the same time, what he said made sense. After all those hundreds of calls and no sales, I knew something had to be wrong.

"Know why I called you to come and see me?" he asked.

"I sure don't, sir."

"Well, son, I've checked up on you. From all I can find out, you're a nice southern boy. You just don't have any business sense."

"Guess not," was the only thing I could say.

To add insult to injury, he took me back to the airport and offered me ten dollars to buy my supper. I declined. "I have enough for my supper," I told him, insulted and hurt. I returned home thinking to myself in the words of the Cub Run whittler: *I guess I'm getting learnt, because I surely got burnt this time!*

The next day I went to the office and called all three employees together. "Folks, the well has run dry," I said. I explained the situation and added, "I'm calling in the dogs because the fox chase is over." I hated to have to let them go, but I had no choice.

Creditors hounded me. My savings, now exhausted, left me without any capital or income. My lawyer urged me to file for bankruptcy, but my Kentucky pride wouldn't let me.

"But it's perfectly legal," he said.

"It may be legal, but it's not right," I answered.

I knew he wanted to help, but I couldn't go his way. I tried to explain my feelings. "My daddy always said that nothing's more disgusting than a man who won't pay his bills. . . . "

"This isn't a case of not paying. . . . "

"Going bankrupt to get out of them is the same as cheating," I said.

"It's not the same at all," he said.

"Maybe not," I answered, "but I can't do it that way."

I contacted every creditor and explained my predicament. "I'll pay you back, in full, every cent, but you'll have to bear with me and ride out the storm with me," I told them. "I'll pick up Coke bottles in the streets if I have to, but I give you my word of honor that I'll pay back every single penny." Every creditor stood with me. It took a long time to pay it all back, but I finally did. Every penny.

Once I cleared that hurdle, I had to find a way to support my family. Several companies had offered me fabulous jobs a year earlier, so I started with them.

One friend, the personnel director of a company, responded typically. "Sorry, Stan, we can't use you," he said. "You're not really interested in going back into the sales business. You're only trying to use us for a nestegg and then you'll launch out on your own again."

"That's not true," I argued. "I had my little fling. It didn't work and I'm through with it."

"Sorry, Stan, but we can't take that chance. We hire people who want to get ahead in the business."

Everywhere I went, the same answer. I had to eat crow. I had held up a good front for three months with expensive suits, lovely offices, and a staff. Yet I couldn't even keep the business going. For a long time I didn't want to admit my circumstances to anyone. It was almost as if, by keeping up a facade, I could change the way things went. But I didn't change anything. Things only got worse. Yet acknowledging my stupidity came hard. The code of the hills says we protect our name. For a man to lose his good name is about the worst thing that can happen.

Meanwhile, we got further and further in debt. Nothing I tried worked out. Carol's parents loaned us the money to make house payments for four months. Finally, Carol went to work. That year (1979) we had a total income of $8,000, and $7,800 of it came from her salary as a teacher.

"We've got to keep the house," she said several times between tears. And being a more realistic person about money than I, she kept saying, "Stan, as long as we've got a roof over our heads, we can make it."

In all the terrible ordeal of those days, Carol was the one constant factor. Her faith in me never wavered. She never complained. And no matter how low I felt, she kept saying, "Stan, honey, we can make it."

At the time I wasn't so sure.

14
A World Record in Twenty-four Hours!

People sometimes ask, "Stan, what was your toughest run?"

I can joke and say, "Every one of them." No two runs are alike. Every run has its own problems and each one demands its toll physically and mentally. When I move my feet along the road, it's the hardest thing so far. I don't just keep doing the same things, for I'm constantly looking for new mountains to climb.

However, one run was the most exhausting of all. It was the 24-hour run I did in September 1979 at the Lovett School in Atlanta.

A year earlier, I had completed the 405-mile run across Georgia, from Chattanooga to the Florida line. That gave me the confidence to believe that I was now ready to break ultramarathon records.

I began reading and finding out what the records were, and in my reading I discovered that the record for the longest distance run in twenty-four hours by an American runner was 133 miles. The world record was 151. I thought about this for several days. After all, I had never run twenty-four hours straight. But then, I reasoned, I had never run the 405 miles before I'd actually tried it. That's how we live, accepting new challenges.

I gathered all the information I could. Most important, the event had to be sanctioned so that, if I beat the existing record, I could legally hold the world title. I contacted groups such as the American Athletic Union, but they told me they didn't get involved in anything of that sort. I knew I needed officials to keep track of the time and I assumed that by working with a reputable organization and reputable people, I would prevent problems after the event.

Finally, I contacted the American Heart Association, and they helped me immensely by announcing the event. They also provided the needed people to enable me to officially qualify if I beat the record.

Two national runners' magazines made references to my upcoming event. Unfortunately, my attempt to run continuously for twenty-four hours couldn't generate nearly as much interest or publicity locally as a 6.2-mile race being held in the area.

I learned that at least three counters would be required because every lap had to be counted and timed. I worked out all the other details so that there would be no question about the facts.

My friends provided the greatest hindrance. Maybe I should have known that. I expected when I talked about running for twenty-four hours straight, people who knew me and my past achievements would encourage me. Instead I got comments like, "You're plain out of your head this time." "You gotta be crazy to try something like that."

A few people said something like, "Why do you want to do a fool thing like that anyway?"

With the American Heart Association behind me I received a lot of pre-publicity.

The run started at 6 P.M. on Monday, September 24. It had been a fairly warm day but by sundown the temperature dropped to 63 and got even colder during the night. The next morning the skies were overcast and remained so the entire time.

Atlanta television station WQXI Channel 11 positioned a helicopter above me when I started the event. From there they took pictures; from time to time it returned for an update. A number of radio stations sent reporters. Even the Kentucky Lung Association got behind the event; their public relations director, Barry Gottschalk, came to help supervise the counters and to see if I was for real. At the start of the race, a number of people joined me, and some ran with me for as long as three hours.

The first hour provided little challenge. I had learned that the secret of endurance is to start slow. I have a theory I call Even Flow of Energy Distribution (EFED). Simply put, it means that I maintain a constant running level. I don't go in spurts. Rather, I expend the same amount of effort throughout the run.

I completed the first hour averaging 7:05 minutes a mile and yet I felt as if I were just creeping along. According to plan I would run three miles (twelve laps), then walk a lap. While walking I would ingest fluids. Then I would resume the run for another three miles. After three hours I would stop. I would soak my feet in ice water, dry them off, cover them with vaseline, rest and begin again. I followed this plan throughout the night.

The air, coming off the Chattahoochee River nearby, became quite chilly and the temperature fell into the 40s.

Every hour a local radio station broadcast an update. TV news carried a report at 11 P.M. After the eleven o'clock news, people streamed into the stadium and cheered me on. Their presence gave me a real lift.

The hours from 1:00 until 4:00 in the morning were the most difficult. Fortunately a few running friends paced me during parts of that lonely time. I wore a sweater, even though I didn't feel cold; my support crew huddled together in a corner of the field, with nothing to do except watch me. As I ran lap after lap in those predawn hours I wished I could just sit there with them and relax and drink coffee.

A few days before I began the run, word reached me that an American named Park Varner had just broken the world record by totalling up 161 miles. That news had caused a last-minute readjustment, but I knew that if I completed the first one hundred miles in less than fifteen hours I had a good chance of beating the record.

When I reached a hundred miles I wanted to know my total time.

"Thirteen hours, twenty minutes," called the timekeeper.

It was an optimistic moment for me because I knew I had a good chance to set a new world's record.

After the sun was up that morning, students from Lovett School gathered and stood all around the field, yelling words of encouragement. Other people, on their way to work, left early so they could stop by and watch me. I remember laughing to myself, *I wonder if they're checking to see if I'm still alive or still running.*

I maintained an even pace for the first hundred miles; almost every mile was clocked at just under eight minutes. Afterward, I felt myself slowing down. I expected to do that.

As I ran on and on, I knew people were cheering, but I didn't hear them. In a strange way I could sense their anticipation as I plunged on toward the record. But it was as though my brains were scrambled, because I concentrated on just one thing: breaking that record. I still had nine hours to go. My thinking began to be confused, but I knew I had energy enough to make it.

Going around the track, around and around and around and around, I eventually lapsed into a hypnotic state.

I ran the entire distance in one direction, my left side leaning into the curve. By the time I had completed a hundred miles my side had begun to throb. Later, people asked me why I didn't change directions.

I said, "I didn't know you could do that."

Somebody always wants to challenge every single record. I tried so hard to make everything exact and to avoid any kind of challenge. I later learned it doesn't matter how careful you are, somebody will always try to prove dishonesty.

My left side throbbed so badly, but I tried not to think about it. I had learned in long-distance running to take my mind off the pain in my body and to go on.

From sunrise until mid-morning I ran alone; then several runners joined me. Their presence picked up my spirits somewhat.

I continued to take fluids and food. Carol bakes me a special kind of carrot cake with ground whole wheat flour, sweetened with fructose. I drank a special liquid that I have concocted, also sweetened with fructose. I also took fructose tablets. All this raises my energy level.

The worst thing, of course, was my feet. They had begun to blister from the constant running. Petroleum jelly oozed out of my socks. I had cut holes in my shoes for additional air to get through. I tried to cut down on the friction.

As the day wore on, hour after hour, I throbbed from my waist down. By noon I asked, *What am I doing here? Why am I continuing to run? This is crazy.* Each time I answered myself: *I said I was going to do it! I told the world I was going to beat this record, and I'm going to do it!*

Throughout the day, students from physical education classes at Lovett School cheered me on. Sometimes as many as one hundred students sat in the bleachers or along the side of the track. They really encouraged me.

Dr. Bob Lathan, a local physician who had checked me regularly, made his last examination at one o'clock in the afternoon. After that I felt my pace grow slower. I was later to learn that for the complete run I averaged eight minutes and thirty-six seconds per mile.

As I moved toward those last five hours I became increasingly weary. I can describe it only by saying I felt as though my legs weighed a ton. Each step was pure torture.

One of my friends, Bill Royston, joined me about three o'clock. He wanted to be with me when I broke the record, and to stay with me till the end. By the time I had completed six hundred laps, almost far enough to set a new record, my running had slowed to a shuffle. The throbbing had become prolonged, stinging pain. My knee caps felt like sticks of dynamite ready to go off.

At 4:40 I was twenty yards from breaking the record. The stadium had filled with people as the news spread that I had a good chance to shatter the record.

The mind can do funny things to a person. When I was within yards of breaking the record, I stopped. My mind had totally fogged. I remember standing there, looking at the imaginary line and yelling at it, "Keep your stupid record!"

I can't explain my actions because I didn't have enough control to know what was going on. I suspect that once I had gotten to a place where I was ready to succeed, I feared success. For some people failure is easier to handle than success.

Later Carol told me that people shouted at me, pleading with me to go on. I couldn't hear them. I didn't hear anything. I had become so hypnotized by the constant running that nothing but silence engulfed me.

Carol ran out onto the track. She said I just stood there crying while staring at the line. I gestured wildly and kept screaming, "Keep your stupid record!"

"Stan, you've got to go on," she pleaded.

"I don't want to go on," I heard myself say.

"You have to, Stan! You're so close to success."

School children ran around me yelling at me, pleading with me to go on, but I scarcely heard them. Then something inside me began to come alive. I took those steps forward and crossed that imaginary line. Suddenly a large bell began to ring somewhere in the bleachers. People really screamed and shouted then. The school bell rang on; I had broken the record!

I still had an hour and twenty minutes to go. I knew then that I wasn't going to quit. It was an eerie kind of feeling. After breaking the record, with each step forward I said to myself, *No one has ever gone this far in twenty-four hours like I'm doing right now.* I was taking steps that no one else had taken before. My mind still didn't function clearly.

Sometime during that last hour Bill Royston told me that I looked at the parking lot and said, "That's the biggest rat I ever saw in my whole life, looking at us."

Bill laughed at the time. I had pointed to a black Volkswagen.

I completed lap 669. That meant 167¼ miles. Voices still yelled, "Go on, Stan! Go on!"

I had one more minute that I could keep running, but I knew that I couldn't take another step. I stopped.

"That's enough," I said, and walked off the track.

I don't know how I even made it off the track. My feet were bleeding, with broken blisters covering the bottoms.

As Dr. Lathan examined me, I begged for medication. "Anything," I said. "Just give me something for the pain."

"Can't do that, Stan," he said as he continued checking me out.

"Just chlorohydrate then," I said. Having been a pharmaceutical salesman I knew chlorohydrate would put me to sleep without having a hangover effect many medications produce. I also knew that with all the excruciating pain in my body, I would never get to sleep without medication.

I pleaded again.

"No, Stan," he said patiently as though talking to a child. In my exhausted and confused state, I suppose I acted like a child. "Your body has to work this out by itself. That's the best thing for you."

I begged him again.

Gently, but firmly he said, "Stan, I can't do that. Too often doctors give out medicines and they only mask symptoms, making sick people feel better than they are. I know you're hurting, but this is nature's way. Let your body heal itself without a lot of medications."

I think Dr. Lathan knew me well enough to know that if he gave me something for the pain, I would start running again too soon and do harm to my body. I finally accepted his advice, but my body still ached.

As he walked away, reporters stuck microphones in my face. Cameramen and amateur photographers crowded in. Questions came, one after another.

"How did it feel that last mile?"

"How did you keep going?"

I hope I answered them properly. I remember very little. I hurt too much.

Finally Carol drove me home. Within an hour the British Broadcasting Company called and interviewed me. I smiled, knowing that I had made world news.

I had taken a decisive step in my career. No one in recorded history had run that far in twenty-four hours. When it came to running, I knew that I could do anything I tried.

But my elation was short-lived. Then came the pain. I went to bed, but I knew I couldn't stop hurting enough to sleep. I had set a world record, but right then I didn't care about anything except escape from the pain.

Because of the pain, I was unable to sleep that night. Carol told me that I screamed out in agony so that she even couldn't sleep. The next morning, by a sheer act of will, I dragged my body out of bed. I knew one principle of ultramarathon running. You have to taper down gradually after a run. I wasn't sure I could follow that principle that morning, however. I could hardly stand, let alone walk. Yet I knew that I had to get moving. To give in to my pain now and lie in bed would only make it worse for myself later.

For the next two weeks, I struggled to recover. Every time I closed my eyes, I could see a black ribbon in a circle. I felt as though I had an inner ear infection and couldn't walk straight or hold my balance.

On that morning after, I tried to go for a walk. I didn't get very far, but I stuck it out for a full hour before coming back inside to rest. Later I walked a second hour. Someone drove me to a health spa and I sat in the whirlpool a while. After more rest, I went out for another hour's walk. Slowly I recovered, but it took two full weeks before I began to feel like myself again. By the end of the third week I could say that I was normal.

I'm convinced that this was the most grueling run I've ever made and the most taxing on me mentally and physically.

Nonetheless, a lot of good things happened. Speaking engagements opened up to me. The Dinah Shore show booked me. I felt my career was finally taking off.

Then came something I could not possibly have foreseen—an attack on my character from a member and record keeper from a national runners' club. He hit my most vulnerable spot. The code of the hills says that a man's good name is his most prized possession. I had been called names before. Some people didn't like me. But no one had ever tried to label me a fraud.

Ignoring the unquestionable reputation and impeccable character of the persons who kept records for the event, this man said I couldn't possibly have run for twenty-four hours and that I had falsified the records. And he didn't make the charges only once. He made them frequently and as vocally as possible.

A friend of mine said, "Stan, this doesn't need to surprise you. As soon as you succeed, you're going to have all kinds of attacks. It's as though people don't want you to succeed. They only want you to fail."

I didn't want to admit that he was right, but I knew he was.

The man charged that we had kept improper records, even though he was not present. He must have spent a lot of money and time trying to convince people that I cheated.

I kept hearing of his attack everywhere I went. I ran in 10k events or marathons and had other runners say to me at the finish: "I stayed alongside you the whole way just to find out for myself if you would really cheat. But you hung in all the way."

I spoke with my lawyer friend, Tyler Dixon, and he advised me to try to forget the man's charges. "I'd ignore it all," he said.

Others said, "The more publicity you give this, the more it will hurt running."

A board member of the runners' club of which the man was a member phoned my friend Jack Mahurin, who had made that first attempt with me to run across Kentucky. (Jack is now chairman of the department of health and physical education at Mississippi State University.) Knowing that Jack and I were no longer running together, he apparently hoped that Jack would give him something more to feed the rumors.

Jack told him, "I know Stan Cottrell and he's honest. He doesn't have to cheat. When he's in shape, he can run me into the ground if he wants to. Check your records. Stan's been running since the '50s, in numerous long-distance events."

The attacks didn't stop, but I learned to ignore them.

Finally, at a national convention of the club, a man said publicly, "I'm sick of all this. You must be talking about a different Stan Cottrell than the one I know. The Stan Cottrell I know is a respected runner, yet it seems as if every time I pick up your newsletter somebody attacks him. It just doesn't add up. Everywhere else he's appreciated and admired. You're the only people who attack him."

Since that speech, I've never heard anything further. Interestingly, one of the charges had been that it is humanly impossible for any man to run 167 miles in twenty-four hours. And, since it is impossible, I had obviously falsified the records. Approximately a year after my record-setting marathon, a man in France beat my record; he ran 169 miles.

When word reached me of the new record, I breathed a sigh of relief. While I would have liked to have held the world record, the fact that someone had broken it proved that my feat was not impossible. I've sometimes wondered what my critic said when he heard about this new record of 169 miles. To my knowledge, no one has ever called it fraudulent!

15
"Ya Done Good, Son"

Over the years I had never given up the idea of completing a run across the state of Kentucky, 146 miles. Somehow it had never worked out. Two weeks after my twenty-four-hour run, I decided it was time to try again or forget it. I called Jack Mahurin.

"You crazy?" he asked. "It's only been two weeks since you broke that twenty-four-hour record. You're not ready for a demanding run like that."

"Sure, I am," I said, confident of my ability and equally confident that I had fully recovered. "Besides, I've still got two more weeks."

"Two more weeks?" he said and laughed. "That's not enough."

"It is for me."

He laughed again. "Count me out. I don't do crazy long runs like that anymore."

I realized then that it was *my* dream, not Jack's. If I ever ran completely across the state, I had to do it alone.

The Kentucky Lung Association agreed to sponsor me. They publicized the event through interviews on TV and radio and in all kinds of newspaper coverage. They even took out a full-page ad in the Louisville paper.

I was 36 years old. In the thirteen years since my first try I had learned a lot about running long distances. I prepared this time—not as much as I would later, but as much as I knew how to then. Lightweight shoes, with ample ventilation, were available; they were an important part of my equipment. I arranged to have a doctor check me along the way. I listened to weather reports. As I was to learn, however, the weatherman is sometimes taken by surprise.

I began this run across Kentucky at 9:00 A.M. on the morning of October 22, 1979. A pleasantly warm 80° with a not-too-high humidity level greeted me. I started the run at a sensible pace and held to it. At every town, people stood by the wayside, yelling greetings and photographing me. Several times I heard loud speakers announcing that I was passing through.

After I had run nearly fifty miles, the weather changed abruptly. Within two and a half hours, the temperature dropped from 80° to 34°. A sudden wind came up and ushered in a cold front. The weather experts hadn't foreseen this. The rain lashed at me, and wouldn't let up; but I kept running. At times I could hardly see where I was going, but I was determined not to be stopped this time.

Waves of dizziness overpowered me and I would almost lose my balance. Then it would pass and I would run on. The rain not only continued to soak me, but my body temperature couldn't adjust; my teeth chattered and I felt shaky. In all the running I had done, I had never felt like that before, and I had gone through plenty of rainstorms. Later, a doctor told me that I was suffering from hypothermia because of the drastic shift in temperature.

I had almost reached the Hart County line, a distance of sixty-five miles, when everything started to spin. I knew I couldn't keep going. Like an idiot I had not brought proper clothing for this kind of weather. I needed Gore-tex clothing and thermal underwear or polypropylene. Instead, I wore only what we call rain shells that keep off the rain but offer little protection.

Finally, I stopped running. Just about then my father pulled up in the pickup five feet away. That was a surprise. I couldn't believe that he had come looking for me.

"C'mon, get in, Son," he said, flinging open the door on my side.

Trying to stand straight, I shuffled toward the truck, taking what seemed like minutes to walk that short distance. On the one hand, I was glad to get in out of the torrential downpour. At the same time, I feared that if I rested I would not be able to get going again.

Once I was inside, Daddy handed me a thermos of hot coffee. "Here, drink some. It'll warm you up.

"You sure are a glutton for punishment," he said, shaking his head. I tried to smile, but I'm not sure it came across that way because the chill had gone through my whole body.

"You all right?"

"Guess so," I said. I still couldn't believe that he had come. I was even more surprised by the next thing he said.

"I've been driving up and down the road the last two hours looking for you."

"You have?" I said. "Thanks."

Knowing that he cared enough to come looking for me in the rain brought a lump to my throat and tears to my eyes. I didn't trust my voice to say anything more. For a few seconds we sat in the pickup. We seemed suspended in that noisy silence, listening to the howling wind and slashing rain.

"Feel like you're going to make it?" he finally asked.

"Dunno."

"This is something nobody counted on, this weather. . . . " And then, as if to encourage me he added: "I'm not supposed to tell you, but you won't believe what a celebration they've got planned for you in Munfordville. I'm going on up ahead and tell them where you are."

"Okay, Daddy."

"Can you make it that far?"

"I'm sure I can," I said, not sure at all, but determined to try as hard as I could.

I got out of the truck and watched Daddy pull back up on the road and drive ahead. Knowing that he would be in Munfordville encouraged me to begin running again. I felt better after resting in the truck.

A mile down the road, the first sign of a celebration appeared. Tommy Joe Turner had parked the Munfordville fire truck, with its red light blazing, beside the road. The state police, with blue lights flashing, parked across the road. "Hey, Stan, we came to meet you! Welcome home!" Tommy Joe called out over the fire truck's loud speaker.

Even though it was pouring rain, very dark and cold, at least a dozen runners huddled together, waiting to join me in running to Munfordville.

That's how we made the next five miles—the police car with flashing blue lights leading the parade, runners all around me, the fire truck bringing up the rear.

By then I had intense pains in my groin, like I had been kicked by a sixteen-hand mule. I winced from the pain, but kept running. I was now traveling over the same stretch of road I had run twenty years earlier when I had bet my friends I could make it from Horse Cave to Munfordville. Reliving that event took my mind off the pain. I kept running.

Eventually I reached the bridge spanning the Green River. From there I could see people lining both sides of the road. As soon as I crossed the bridge, the school band struck up a march.

"Biggest thing that's happened in Hart County since the hanging of Custer Gardiner," one of the runners said. That legendary hanging supposedly brought out more people than anything in our town's history. To compare this with it was a high compliment.

As soon as I reached Munfordville, someone pulled on my arm, and before I knew it I was inside radio station WLOC. There Jim Berry, the owner and a longtime friend, greeted me. Next to him stood Bob Chambliss, the president of the local bank and president of the Chamber of Commerce. The room was packed with people. Momma and Daddy were there, too, to be interviewed.

Frankly, I don't remember an awful lot. I smiled and tried to sound alert, but I was so sick I hardly knew what was happening around me. Someone gave me a dry T-shirt and I changed quickly. Just that little change made me feel better.

Once or twice I looked up and noticed that our local doctor, Mayer Speevak, stared oddly at me. He told me later that he detected that I was already suffering from basic hypothermia.

For a few minutes I felt oblivious to the pain because Jim Berry was telling people not about me, but about my father. Daddy had become widely known and respected in the community. Three times he had run for county judge, and though he hadn't won, the town folk looked up to him. After praising Dad, Jim handed Mom flowers, and various people presented me with plaques and awards.

I looked up at the station clock, and, seeing that it was nearly 9:00 P.M., I felt I had to get back on the road. Eventually the celebration broke up and I started to run again.

But I could hardly run. The cold, drenching rain had taken its toll and I felt stiffer than I ever had in my life. *I'll limber up as I run some more,* I said to myself, hoping that I spoke the truth. My head ached, and the pain in my groin started again.

Leaving Munfordville, I ran toward Bonnieville. Nausea hit me and several times I felt as though I were going to pass out. Barry Gottschalk, one of the men with me, said, "Stan, let's take a break."

"I'd really like just a cup of hot tea," I said.

We came to a truckstop at the outskirts of Bonnieville, six miles from Munfordville, and went inside. While waiting for some tea, I had to fight just to remain conscious. It would have been so easy to collapse. Barry kept talking and I mumbled in reply each time, not sure what he said or caring very much. I felt I was becoming disoriented, not even sure for a few seconds where I was. I gulped down the tea and said, "Another, please."

The tea seemed to settle my stomach a little and I felt better. "Let's just sit a little," I said.

Half an hour later we left the truckstop and I hobbled out to the road. After but a half dozen steps I stopped. "I can't run," I said. I could hardly stand.

We had a back-up van with us and I think they led me to it; I'm not sure if I passed out or not. No matter what people were saying around me, I kept saying "That's fine."

"Let's wait another hour and then try again, Stan."

"That's fine."

"No, don't you think it would be better if we waited until first light?"

"That's fine."

Finally someone had enough sense to say, "He can't run any more tonight. Let's take him to his folks' place and then we can start out early in the morning, when he's had a chance to rest up a little."

They took me to Daddy's place outside of Munfordville. Daddy looked at me while they spoke about starting out in the morning. "Fellas," he said, "it would be foolish for him to go on. Right now his health is more important than running across the state."

As sick as I was, it made me feel so good to hear Daddy talk that way. "The Cottrell in him wants to keep going, but I'm going to step in here and just say that it would kill him to keep going. No one knew about the rainstorm. He did everything he knew."

He turned to me and said, "Ya done good, Son."

I smiled at him. In all my life I had never heard him say those words to me.

Ya done good, Son. In my head I heard his voice speaking those words over and over.

"You got nothing to be ashamed of," he added, "and I don't want you to go hurting yourself."

I gave in. I didn't complete my goal of 146 miles across Kentucky. I had actually run a total of only 82.

I lay in bed at home for two full days, just recovering. Later the doctor said that those cups of tea had prevented my going into shock.

Surprisingly, I had no sense of failure that time. Daddy had said I had "done good."

He asked me, "You goin' to hang it up?"

"No, Daddy. I'll be back. I learned a lot with this run. The next time I'll be prepared."

Daddy kind of smiled. He may have been thinking of something he had taught me a long time ago: Cottrells never 'mit. All he said was, "Eee-ehh."

16

"I'm Awful Proud of Him"

Hart County declared it "Stan Cottrell Day" and planned a big celebration. It was the end of November 1979, just a month after my second try at running across Kentucky. I really felt honored. But not just for my sake; I wanted it to be a day to honor Daddy as well.

Daddy had kept the pledge he made in 1961 to never drink again. But more than not drinking, he changed in a lot of ways. He got his life in order and began to prosper. Besides the gas station, he ran a used car lot and got involved in a number of other projects, investing and speculating, as well as local politics.

When I went home, one of the first things my father did was to show me his closet. "Got two suits," he said. "New ones."

"Two?" I said, and looked at them.

First of all, Daddy just didn't buy suits. Most of the time he walked around in his bib overalls. As we stood in his bedroom, we talked a little about Stan Cottrell Day festivities that were to start that evening.

"Daddy," I said, "I want you to know that this is as much for you as it is for me."

He turned to the suits and pulled the tan corduroy out. "You think this'll be good enough for things tonight?"

"Daddy, I wouldn't care if you came in dung-smeared overalls and barefoot. I just want to have you there."

"Just wanted to be sure."

"It's fine," I told him.

"You sure I won't embarrass you with this?"

"Embarrass me?" I had never considered the idea. "You couldn't do that."

I felt so excited about his being there. To know that he had even bought a suit just for the occasion delighted me even more.

I talked to him about my proposed run across America. We had been talking about it for months and he knew how hard I had been working trying to get sponsors and set up all the details.

"What's the other suit for?" I asked. I pulled it out so I could appraise the three-piece, dark blue suit. "Looks like a first class businessman's outfit."

"I'm saving that for something special," he answered.

"What's that?" I asked, although I felt I already knew.

"Something special," he said and put it away. But he didn't move quite fast enough. I caught a gleam in his eye and I knew then that he planned to be in San Francisco and wear that suit when I finished my run across America.

Everything went wonderful that day. People called or came by. I could hardly wait for the big event which started at seven. My brother Harold and my sisters were there. The whole family had come together and everything was going so smoothly.

About an hour before we were to leave, Dad came through the house wearing his old clothes with his fox horn hanging on his shoulder. My surprise must have shown and I blurted out, "What—where are you going now? Everything starts in an hour."

"Don't think I'll go tonight." He walked on through the house and out the back door. I could hear him calling his hounds. He was going hunting.

I sat down, unable to say a word. I could see it all before my eyes. Graduation time all over again. All the preparation, all the expectation and then Daddy's walking out at the last minute.

"I'll go talk to him," Harold said.

"No," I said. "I want him only if *he* wants to come on his own."

Harold sat down, trying to say the words to encourage me. So did the rest of the family. But it didn't matter. He had let me down again. In an effort to control myself I yelled, "Momma, you'd better be there!"

Of course, she'd be there and she wisely said nothing.

The minutes ticked by and I went to change clothes. It didn't matter anymore what went on. He had ruined it all for me, just as he did at my college graduation.

We left home at 7:30 and went to Munfordville's country club-type meeting place at Rowletts. People came in carrying plaques, small gifts, and letters. I smiled, trying to enter into the spirit of the evening. And, of course, being around the people helped lift my spirits.

At 7:45 I happened to look up. Then I saw him. My father stood just inside the door for a minute. He was wearing the tan corduroy suit I had seen only hours earlier. In his arm he carried a basket he had made.

I couldn't hold back the tears. I ran past all the tables and around to him. I wanted to scream and shout and yell. Now the whole evening had changed. Someone grabbed him by the arm and before I knew it, both of us were at the head table.

Later, various people got up and made speeches of all kinds. They gave me the gifts I had seen earlier. A number of old friends had gone together and bought me a fine quality overcoat. A state legislator presented me with a petition from the senate proclaiming the day as "Stan Cottrell Day."

Then Jim Berry asked Daddy to make a speech.

Daddy stood up and started talking. "This boy of mine has defeated the odds. I've watched him overcome all the obstacles and he did it. To be truthful, I didn't think he'd make it a lot of times. But he proved me wrong. He says now he's going to run clear across the entire United States. This time I'm listening to him."

A number of things went on in me right then. Suddenly, all the pain and all the disappointment vanished. Over the years I had made excuses for him and thought I had forgiven him. But that night as I sat and listened to my father speak about me, all the anger and resentment vanished.

I was also thinking of that run across the United States. I was going to make him even more proud of me. When I would cross that finish line in San Francisco, he'd stand there with pride. I could visualize him saying to someone, "That's my son. That's Stanley Cottrell, Jr."

As Dad finished his speech, he turned and picked up the basket he had brought with him. With one hand he reached out to shake my hand and with the other he handed me the basket. "Son, hitch your wagon to a star," he said, and sat down.

People recognized Daddy as one of the best basket makers around. In fact, he had often been asked to demonstrate his basket making at Mammoth Cave, a big tourist attraction nearby. Folk would come from far and near to buy his baskets woven from white oak that Daddy carefully prepared himself.

The basket he gave me was like all the rest he had made—top quality. I took it and thanked him, hardly able to say anything else. Then other gifts came and the evening climaxed on a wonderful, happy note. Daddy *was* proud of me. And I was proud of my daddy, too.

Stan Cottrell Day was a wonderful celebration, and it hadn't come any too soon. Less than two months later, on January 10, 1980, I called home to talk to Momma.

"Your Dad's not been feeling too good lately. A little under the weather, I guess," she said.

The previous January he had come down with asthma and I wondered if he had had another attack.

"Not sure," Momma said. "He can't lie down, so he sits up all night and rests a little, but not much."

"Do you think it's serious?"

"We checked him into the hospital today," she said, her voice steady.

"Hospital?" I echoed. I knew then that it had to be serious. Dad had always refused to go to hospitals for any reason.

"Your daddy refused to go, but we finally took him."

"You want me to come up there?" I asked.

"I don't think so, Son. If he gets worse, I'll let you know."

Daddy never came out of the hospital. On January 19, I drove to Kentucky and spent the entire next morning at the hospital with him. When I walked in, he lay quietly in his hospital gown, a plug of tobacco in his mouth. Every few minutes he leaned over and spit.

"You think you ought to be doing that in a hospital?" I asked.

"I'll do anything I please here," he said and spit again.

"But you can't do that in a hospital."

"Well, I do!" he said. That settled that.

We talked about his condition. Dad told me that the doctors couldn't find out the cause of his problem. It was a small county hospital with limited facilities. His temperature shot up and then went down. He had a lot of pain, but not constant. (Later they discovered that it was caused by his kidneys.)

As we talked, I noticed a strange thing. Years earlier he had bought a cross on a chain at an auction. He was wearing it around his neck now and all the time we talked, he kept fingering the cross, almost as if it were a rosary.

I looked at the cross and, I suppose out of embarrassment as much as anything, said, "A man who doesn't put God first in his life is really missing the boat, isn't he?"

Daddy looked straight at me. "If a man doesn't put Christ first, he's a fool."

Just then the other patient in the semiprivate room walked in. "Oh, sorry," he said, "didn't realize you had a visitor." He turned to walk away.

"Naw, come on in," Dad said. "This is my son."

"This the runner you been telling me about?"

Dad nodded. The man came over and shook my hand. "Your dad's been telling me an awful lot about you."

"Yeah, and I'm awful proud of him, too," Daddy said.

I could hardly believe what I was hearing. Even though he had said that only a few weeks earlier, it touched me that he'd been telling his roommate the same thing.

Dad and I went back to our conversation. He talked to me about all the others—my sisters Pam, Debby, Mary and Shirley, and even

Harold. As he talked about each one, he'd say something like, "I love that girl."

In all my life I had never heard my father use the word *love.* It shocked and pleased me. But I kept wanting him to say the same about me. He didn't. I don't think he knew how. But, in his self-conscious way I think he wanted me to know that he loved me, too.

As we talked he mentioned the way he was feeling about a particular situation in the family.

"You know, Daddy, I understand how you feel," I said. "As I get older, I realize that sometimes we Cottrells have the right intention, but don't always have the right method."

He stared a minute and then said, "Eee-ehh" in agreement.

Just then two nurses came into the room. "We need to do some work on him now," one said. Since I had been with him all morning, I mumbled something about leaving.

"Thanks for coming to see me," he said. His words hit me as another shock wave. Never in his life had he thanked me for anything. I knew that what he was saying now was taking real effort on his part.

He held out his hand to me. I started to shake it and then, impulsively, I pushed it away. "I'd rather have a hug," I said. I didn't wait for him to say anything. I just grabbed him. We held each other a few seconds and then I pulled away.

"Bye, Dad," I said and left the room.

I got all the way to the parking lot and then I had a sudden feeling that I would never see my father alive again. Turning, I ran back into the building and to his room.

As I pushed the door open, two nurses and two doctors were gathered around him. Dad sat in the same position, still fingering the cross. He looked at me, smiled and waved.

I smiled back and moved on.

I knew then that I had done everything I could for him in life. Even though all the words that needed saying hadn't been spoken, we had communicated on a level I had never thought possible before.

All the way back to the house, I kept seeing him fingering that cross and smiling back at me.

On January 27, Momma called. Her voice peaceful and quiet, she said, "I want you to be strong, Stanley, but your daddy just passed away. He didn't suffer. It was very easy."

I broke into tears, stunned, shocked, sad. Yet I had known it was coming. I realized then, more than ever, that on that last morning together he had expressed his feeling the best he could, that he loved me and really was proud of me.

At the funeral, the one thing I remember most of all was something Momma did. As we filed past the casket, she took that cross on the chain and placed it inside his hand. Dad was wearing the second suit. Watching her do that brought a deep level of peace to me. I didn't understand much about God at the time. But one thing for sure, my daddy did.

17
Run Across America? Why Not?

Resting on your laurels can be a prickly thing. I had assumed that my successful run across Georgia and my record-setting twenty-four-hour run would have thrust me into the limelight. I imagined that with the publicity given these events I would be known all over the United States.

After running Georgia I eagerly looked for due recognition in the pages of one of the leading running magazines. But they gave my accomplishment all of a *full paragraph.* So much for national recognition! It was then that I realized that one run doesn't do much for a person any more than one boxing victory or one no-hit shutout.

But one good thing did come out of the 405-mile Georgia run: I knew that I could run long distances. Failing to complete the Kentucky run didn't shake that confidence.

People kept bugging me about my next run.

"Which state you going to run across next?" they asked. "Why not try Texas? That's a big state." Another person suggested running the length of the East Coast, from Maine to the tip of Florida.

I had thought of all of these, and a lot more. Actually I had begun thinking about running across the entire United States, but it was such an overwhelming idea that I could hardly comprehend it. Yet the idea nagged me and wouldn't quit.

In my research I had discovered that at least ten people had run across the United States before 1980. The shortest recorded time for the coast-to-coast trip was fifty-three days. I decided right then that if I made the run I would do it in less than fifty days.

Slowly, the determination grew. But I wanted to do everything right. I would have to line up sponsors all by myself. I needed information on how to document the run. And I also had to give a lot of serious thought to my ability. I finally reasoned that I would have to average sixty miles a day in order to break the record. I would do that by running as many as fifty-three miles and finish the day by walking the last six or seven.

I approach all of my long distance runs now with what I call EFED—Even Flow of Energy Distribution. By 1980 I had perfected this approach beyond the method I used on the twenty-four-hour run. I made plans to run across America in this way: run fifteen minutes, walk five minutes, run fifteen minutes, walk five minutes, run fifteen. . . . Every three hours I would stop and rest for approximately an hour, at which time I would take nourishment and catch some rest or a rubdown. I figured that by doing it this way I could run the 3,100 miles from New York City to San Francisco in fifty days or less.

Working out the details for this run required eight months. I had to contact the department of transportation of each state where I would be running. We procured county maps as well as state maps, compiled information about road elevations, expected temperatures, routes, and exact distances between points. Also, we contacted the Guinness people to find out precisely what they required for documentation, because this would be another run for the record.

While that went on, I tackled the financing. I wrote letters and called seven hundred different companies. Every one of them turned me down. They had never heard of such an idea and they couldn't see the value in sponsoring such a bizarre stunt.

If there hadn't been the fanatical drive in me that refused to give up, I would have quit then. It would have been easy to say, "I just can't get the backing." But I had committed myself to a run across America and I wouldn't let go of the idea.

One day a neighbor, a good friend, called and asked if I'd go for a run with him. He and I had run together in the past so that wasn't unusual.

"I wanted to talk to you about something, Stan," he said through his irregular breathing as we started up a hill.

"Anything," I said. "We're friends."

"You know we love you—you and Carol and the kids—and we've known you several years." I let him talk on, wondering what he was leading up to. Then it came. "Stan," he said, "this running has become an obsession with you."

"I suppose you could call it that."

"I'd like you to get professional help," he said.

For a moment I thought he meant a professional fund raiser. He quickly clarified his meaning. "I'm concerned about you. Real concerned, Stan."

"I'm okay—"

"Look, Stan," he went on. "I know things are tight for you right now. So if you'll go to any counselor, I'll pay the bill. You won't ever have to pay me back."

"That's nice of you, but. . . . "

"*And* maybe he can help you give up this crazy running and get your life back to normal again."

I thanked him as politely as I could. I knew it would do no good to argue with him. But my stomach tightened up inside. I could hear the echo of my old school principal in his words. I could hear the sneers from dozens of others. It only made me more determined.

After I had told my father what I planned to do, and he had said publicly that he believed I could do it, that run *had* become an obsession. *I had to do it.* More than once I said to myself: *I may die at the end of the run, but I'll complete it.*

In the meantime I kept on sending out proposals and still nothing happened. I didn't lose hope though. And one day the door finally opened. An ultramarathoner, Dave McGillvray, who had once run completely across the United States, was watching the Boston Celtics play one night. With him were two executives from Keds, the shoe company. They were talking about a running shoe they had developed and planned to market shortly.

Dave knew of my plans to run across America; I had asked him hundreds of questions. That night he did one of the kindest and most unselfish things. He told the men about my planned run and said: "I think you ought to talk to Stan Cottrell."

Within days the Keds people had contacted me and, although they didn't provide as much as I had hoped, they offered enough to cover most of the expenses.

The next day I contacted the people at Ben Gay and as soon as I told them about Keds they made a commitment to help me. Although theirs was a smaller amount, they kept their word. When I ran across the United States, Keds and Ben Gay were my two national sponsors.

At noon on May 16, 1980—after a press conference and all kinds of national publicity—I left New York City on the first leg of what was to be called The Great American Friendship Run.

As I headed toward the Holland Tunnel, I laughed to myself as I remembered the conversation only a few days before. I had called and asked the Port Authority of New York if they would close the Holland Tunnel so that I could run through it. The Holland Tunnel carries thousands of cars daily, between the city and New Jersey.

"Close the Tunnel?" came the reply. The surprise in his voice made me realize that he thought he had some mental case on his hands.

"Maybe just one lane then," I said. "at noon."

"At noon? It's busy at that time of day," he said.

I kept talking and explained what was happening. When I paused he said, "You're really serious, aren't you?"

"Absolutely, sir," I said.

"I don't know," he finally answered. "Let me get back to you in a day or two."

Two days later I called back and he said, "You got it!" I was glad because otherwise I would have added an additional twenty miles to my run.

I started off, followed by well-wishers, representatives from my sponsors, curiosity seekers, and a lot of media people. A number of runners from the New York-New Jersey area ran right with me. I completed forty-five miles that day and many of those runners stayed right with me.

My road crew consisted of Tommy, who drove the van carrying necessary clothing and supplies, Greg, who handled the media relations along the way, and Cliff, my road manager. We had another one or two guys with us part of the time to spell Tommy at the wheel, to wash clothes, or keep records.

Just as in the run across Georgia, I had unusual experiences. The first odd one occurred in Pennsylvania where a woman pulled up beside me and said, "Young man, you can't do this to yourself."

"I'm fine, ma'am, just fine."

"You'll kill yourself," she insisted.

"Thank you, ma'am, but I'm all right."

"I've got a spare room at my house with covers pulled back, a lot of good nourishing food and fresh orange juice. I want you to stop this crazy thing right now and rest your body."

"Can't do that, ma'am."

"You're going to die if you don't stop."

She kept babbling away, absolutely sincere. Finally I said, "Look, in ten minutes I'll stop for a break. You got any of that juice in the car?"

"Of course!"

"Then I'll have a drink of juice with you. But I can't stop the run."

When I reached Ohio, a man who worked for a multi-level sales organization ran up beside me and tried to recruit me.

"You'd make a wonderful distributor," he said.

I laughed. "Got enough to do just running."

He didn't give up. For five days he ran with me part of the way, determined to sign me up. He didn't get me, but he got a workout. He would run at least ten miles with me each day and the next day he'd be back out there. He had persistence.

In the Midwest one woman offered to hitch up two horses and follow behind. "It would be much more comfortable for your drive on horseback than following in a van," she said.

We declined her offer.

In Kansas we encountered the prevailing westerlies in full force. As soon as I hit Route 36 in northern Kansas I felt those headwinds and they didn't let up for twelve straight days.

One day we rested at a truck stop for coffee. I asked the folks: "Are these winds exceptionally heavy today?"

They looked at each other and agreed: "No, guess they're about the same as always."

After battling against them a couple of days I had the van pull in front of me, going very slowly. I tried to stay back far enough to keep my knees about six inches from the van. That meant I hit the bumper numerous times. I would yell at my driver Tommy, "Just one mile faster" or "Slow down one mile." If Tommy got too far ahead, my running was nearly impossible; I was like a bird, flapping its wings but not moving. The run across Kansas was pure torture. But I was to learn that one other stretch of the road would be worse.

Every day I would meet people along the road. The farther west I got the more the news media made something out of it. From being skeptical at first, they started cheering and encouraging me. Sometimes I would find people set up for a picnic, waiting for me to come along. I would often stop, shake hands, even sign autographs. They always seemed so surprised that I'd stop. What they didn't know is that those pauses and the talking just picked up my spirits and gave me the incentive to run even more.

In Colorado, we asked folks about the roads. Even though we had all kinds of maps, each day we asked locals for their advice. The people advised us to go through Rabbit Ear Pass to Steamboat Pass. "It'll save you twenty miles," one person said.

That's the way we went. I wish we hadn't. The road wound and wound, and dwindled down to little more than a dirt road along the escarpment. I hit snow up to my ankles. I was scared—scared for myself and for our top-heavy van. I feared it would go off the ledge of those narrow curves.

Somehow we made it. But after that I asked a lot more questions before taking any shortcuts.

Physically, by the time I reached the Rockies, I didn't know how I could make each day. I would wake up in the morning ready to quit. After each day's run, reporters quizzed me and interviewed me; often I would find them waiting for me in the morning. Some mornings I actually hobbled because of the stiffness and soreness.

I always consumed plenty of a special drink with my breakfast each day. It's called FRED—Fluid Replacement Energy Drink—and was patented by Dr. Richard Ecker of Chicago. Containing fructose, citric acid, magnesium, potassium and other minerals, FRED is rapidly absorbed into the body; it puts back the essential electrolytes into the body.

After breakfast I would resume the run. I should say "shuffle" for that is literally how fast I could move many days when I just started out.

I planned to shuffle along for about thirty minutes so that my leg muscles could limber up. Most days I didn't think they would ever limber up; but somehow they did. Within half an hour I'd be gently jogging, slowly picking up speed.

At times I felt totally numb, as if I were outside my own body, looking down at a mechanical being that was moving along by sheer willpower. Sometimes the pain became so bad, I must have mentally blanked out, but I kept on running. On several occasions, as much as three hours elapsed and yet I had no recollection of anything happening. I just kept moving.

When I reached Lake Tahoe I was joined by a national entertainment celebrity, Willie Nelson. He came out to meet me, dressed in shorts and T-shirt, and we ran along together; I enjoyed his company immensely. Up ahead I saw a pay phone.

"Willie, I've got a big favor to ask you," I said. Then I told him about my friends in Munfordville, especially Jim Berry and his radio station. "I'd like to call Jim right now and let him interview you."

He chuckled and said, "Why not?"

I stopped, called collect, and said to Jim, "I've got a great man here beside me and I think you'd love to interview him." For fifteen minutes he interviewed Willie on tape, and folks tell me he's played it a lot of times back there in Munfordville.

I smiled as I looked ahead and saw Willie Nelson's limo waiting and my support crew parked a distance behind us.

The next day I ran from Lake Tahoe toward Sacramento. Thirty-four miles of it was downhill and I coasted along effortlessly. I knew that running downhill for long periods of time puts an awful strain on the body, and so I was prepared somewhat for the beating this gave me.

The following morning I was one massive throb from my waist to my toes. I felt as though a thousand hypodermic needles were piercing each hip. It was the worst pain I have ever experienced in running and I seriously thought the run was going to have to stop right there. Compared with running that day after thirty-four miles of downhill running, bucking the headwinds in Kansas had been a piece of cake.

I counted up slightly more than thirty miles that day and was thankful to have done that much. The next two days I was able to return to my average of fifty miles so that on July 3 I had but twenty-four miles to go.

During the final days of my run I thought a lot about Daddy. I would run along and carry on a conversation with him. "Daddy, if you can hear me, I want you to know I'm going to make it." I said words like that over and over. In my head, I sorted out a lot of my feelings toward my father. I felt more love toward him and peace toward myself than I ever had before. *I don't ever have to prove anything to anybody anymore,* I told myself. Knowing that I was going to complete the run helped me shake those thoughts of inadequacy I'd had all of my life.

As I ran toward the finish line I kept saying to myself, *Daddy, I did it! I did it for you!* I sprinted those last five miles, faster than I needed to run. But I couldn't hold back.

When I reached the finish line, Jim Berry stood at the head of a delegation that included Bob Chambliss, the local banker, Mom, Carol, and lots of Kentucky friends. I saw Momma's face and it seemed as if Daddy stood next to her. Tears streamed down my cheeks. It was not just the release from finishing the run; I knew why the tears flowed. They were a message between Daddy and me.

You believed me, Daddy! You believed me! And see, I didn't let you down.

18
"Oh God, I'm So Despicable!"

After the run across America I honestly thought I was ready to go to Hollywood. With all the attention I was getting in the newspapers and TV and radio, I thought I had it made. Wherever I would go it seemed, someone wanted my autograph.

But, of course, as I've already shared, nothing happened. Instead, I got further in debt and the frustration of it all was very hard on our marriage.

As so many men do who are wrapped up in making money, I had ignored the *most* important person to me, my wife. She tried to reach out to me, but I was always either away, or too busy, or too tired. For seven years our marriage had deteriorated. We talked, but our words remained more and more on the surface. I began to snap at her and felt irritable most of the time I was home.

What I didn't know was that Carol had once confided in her mother that she didn't know if she could go on much longer.

Her mom told her, "Carol, you can't come home. When you married Stan, you promised for better or for worse and you're going to stick with him."

"I'm not sure I can stand much more," Carol said.

"You can take it, Carol. You have to."

"I just don't know," she said.

"Stan doesn't beat you or spend his money on liquor," her mom insisted. "You're going to hang in there. Marriage is a matter of commitment, not convenience."

Carol determined that, no matter what, she would never leave me. She didn't have a lot of happy days after that, but she made up her mind that she *had* truly married me "for better, for worse."

During those months after the run across America things definitely grew *worse.* There were indiscretions about which the less said the better. Suffice it to say, the patience and perseverance of Carol—plus a few well-directed kicks to the seat of my pants by Tyler—pulled the whole family through the ordeal and uncertainty of this period of our lives.

A good bit of this time I felt dirty, no good, inadequate, and highly insecure. When I would have a particularly frustrating day, I called it an "LSD day"—I would have to be on dope to accept the kind of deal presented me and the people would have to be on dope to offer me such a deal!

In the midst of just such a day I returned home to be confronted by an intense and determined Carol. She looked me in the eyes and said, "Stan, somewhere along the line I evidently have failed you, and failed you miserably."

She went on. "I don't mind telling you that I've hurt a lot these years. My insides are ripping right now. But I'll get over it. We've been married nine years and I'm not about to throw away all that time I've invested with you. We can work through this with God's help. We've worked through a lot, and we can work through this."

I wasn't so sure. Had I gone beyond the point of no return? My domestic troubles were only one of my concerns. During this time people were coming to me with every kind of offer, everything from book and movie contracts to requests that I sell vitamins, shoes, T-shirts, every conceivable gadget for runners, or promote various organizations. None of these deals worked out. Though dozens of them had fallen apart, I still hoped that the right deal would come my way.

My lawyer and friend, Tyler Dixon, kept a drawer filled with manila folders containing these deals and one day I walked into his office, confident at last that I had a viable offer. Under my arm I carried nine new folders. I handed them to Tyler.

He took them, but he didn't even look at them. Instead, he shoved them across the desk. "They're no good, Stan," he said. "They're going to fail just like all the others."

"How do you know? You haven't even looked at them."

"I don't have to look at them. They're going to fail like all the rest."

For a moment I stared at Tyler. He's about my height, stockier, with brown hair and very intense blue eyes. When Tyler speaks, I've learned to look at his eyes. I could see both the anger and the intensity with which he was trying to say something to me. "But these are different—just look at them," I pleaded.

"Stan, you've got your priorities all wrong, and until you get your priorities straight, everything is going to fail."

"What do you mean 'priorities all wrong'?" I started to tell him how hard I had worked, and concern for my family topped my list.

He stopped me cold. "Stan, don't you realize that God is closing every door on you? He's going to continue closing every door until He gets your attention." His chin jutted forward and he said, "Stan, how many more doors is He going to close before you wake up and start listening?

"How long is God going to have to keep kicking you on the shins? Until He finally breaks your legs?"

"Let's not get into that! Let's don't get business and God all mixed up."

"Stan," he said slowly, "those projects probably look good and maybe they are, but they've got the stamp of failure on them. I'm convinced that nothing you do is going to succeed until you get your life right with God."

"Oh, come on, Tyler," I begged again.

"Stan," he said. "There's only one way that I'll look through these and advise you."

I flashed my best smile at him, deciding he had finally come around to my way of thinking.

"That is, if you go to church with me."

"Go to church with you?"

"That's right. That's my condition. They are having a week-long special seminar in Atlanta. I'd like you to go Monday night."

He talked on and I sat there, staring first into space and then at the floor, thinking to myself, *I can't believe this religious fanatic talking to me like this.*

Like the good lawyer he is, Tyler hammered away at me. It finally dawned on me that he meant his single condition: attend a religious service or else. As I thought about it, I decided one experience ought not to be too bad.

"Okay, Tyler, I'll be at the seminar Monday night."

"Don't let something else turn up at the last minute," he said.

I laughed then and so did Tyler. He knew me well and if he hadn't already made me promise to come, I would quite likely have had an important business meeting come up on Monday night.

I didn't know it, but Carol had undergone a change. She had long been a Christian, but in meeting and marrying me she had swerved from the course. When our life together got really bad, she made a fresh commitment of her life to God. She started attending church regularly but she didn't nag me to go. As long as she didn't try to force me to go, I didn't mind her going.

Then, only weeks before Tyler cornered me, Carol and three neighbors began meeting together three times a week. We were living on the north side of Atlanta and all three of those friends attended First Baptist Church in Atlanta where Carol had started attending.

As they prayed together, they spent a lot of their time in prayer for me, asking God to help me get my life straight with Him.

Monday night came, and instead of Tyler showing up at my house he sent a fellow named Bruce Lorick. I had known Bruce a long time and always thought of him as a little strange. He and I had traveled together on business for a short time. Every time we stopped he passed out tracts and talked to people about Jesus Christ. I always felt uncomfortable and tried to avoid being in public places with him when I could.

Several times when we traveled together we would be in a town and he would spot a religious bookstore. "Stan, let's stop for a minute," he would say. "I need to run into that bookstore."

He never spent less than twenty dollars. I didn't say anything to him, but I thought he was half crazy.

I told Carol once, "Can you believe that idiot? He spends maybe $80 a month. That's $800—even a thousand a year. I can't believe he's quite right in the head because he gives all those books and pamphlets away—free."

Wisely, Carol said nothing when I had those tirades.

On that Monday evening, I opened the door to Bruce. It angered me to see him, but I smiled anyway.

"Tyler sent me to take you to the seminar," he said. "I've even paid your fee."

"You—" and I let go with a string of profanity, angry that he planned to drive me.

Bruce smiled and said, "May I come in?"

As I let him in, I yelled, "You religious do-gooders, you don't need to haul me off to some churchy function."

"We weren't trying to haul you off. . . . "

"Listen, Mr. God Man, I'll show you. . . . " I was ready to use his coming as an excuse not to go.

Carol sensed what was happening so she stepped in and smoothed out everything. We rode to downtown Atlanta with Bruce.

I was mean to poor Bruce but I was also mad. They had ganged up on me and I didn't like it. I had enough talk about Jesus Christ from Carol and I didn't need it from others, too.

As soon as I sat down in the auditorium I saw Tyler sitting a few rows from us. I waved at him so that he would know I had kept my promise.

I kept my promise by going to the seminar. And that's all I had promised. I decided to outsmart them. One of the unique things about me is that when I decide to sleep I can doze off anywhere. As soon as the teaching began I closed my eyes and went to sleep.

After the service, Bruce said, "What a great seminar! Didn't you get a lot out of it?"

"I came just like everybody's pushing me to do," I said, "but let me tell you something. I fixed you! I went to sleep! I slept through almost all of that preaching and didn't hear anything the man said. What do you think of that?"

Bruce laughed. "Well, Stan," he said, "I guess we'll just have to pray for you, so that the next time you won't be so sleepy."

"Next time? There's not going to be any next time."

Yet there were other times. Two weeks later, and on my own, for reasons I couldn't even explain to myself I went to the First Baptist Church where Tyler was a member. Wisely, no one pushed me. No one asked why. I simply went to church and I didn't talk about it to anyone.

In the weeks that followed, every one of those nine projects blew up in my face. No matter how hard I worked, none of them clicked. I couldn't understand it.

Then I began to feel like my father when he kept drilling holes trying to strike oil. He drilled dry bores thirty times and each time he threw himself into the drilling with as much enthusiasm as he had at the beginning.

But I wasn't Daddy. I kept trying and each time it came out empty. I couldn't pretend success, even though I tried. Events forced me to look closely at myself. I thought I was the great Stan Cottrell, top businessman, but not a penny was coming in. Worse, there were not even any prospects. When I tried to get a job, everybody turned me down.

"You want to use us for a springboard so that when you're out of debt, you'll go back into running or trying to start your own business," they would say. No matter how much I denied those statements, I couldn't convince anyone to hire me.

I had made Daddy proud of me when I finally completed my first long-distance run across Georgia. He had also been proud of me when I attempted my second run across Kentucky, even though I didn't make it all the way. And he would have been proud of me in completing the run across America. But those negative voices from the past, which I thought I had stilled once and for all, returned to haunt me. I had nothing now. Even though he was dead, I could hear Daddy say to me: "Can't you do anything right?"

I feared. Was I going to turn out like Uncle Roy after all—a loser?

My parents had drilled the code of the hills into me. And where I lived, people always said, "If a man can't properly take care of his wife and kids, he's nothing."

Carol's teaching job solved one problem: we had money coming in. At the same time, it caused me a great problem. That same old teaching from my childhood only compounded the fact of my failure. My being without an income forced my wife to go to work to support me, showing me and the world that I was not only a failure, but lazy as well.

"I'm nothing," I wailed over and over while alone. I went for my daily runs, but often cut them short. Running didn't seem to matter much. Nothing did. I hated myself and every failure of the past haunted me. I slept poorly, ate badly, and answered mostly in monosyllables.

I felt as if I had fallen from the top of the highest mountain and lay writhing in pain at the bottom. I didn't have the strength to try to climb back up.

My thinking became so confused and twisted that I knew I had to do something. I couldn't keep on. I thought of suicide, but it passed. Then I thought of leaving. *If I can just get out of here, I'll start over again. Forget all my crazy dreams and just be like everyone else. Then maybe I can have peace and enjoy life again.*

One morning while driving along the expressway, I made that decision. And, immediately, I felt at peace. I'd leave Carol and the children. I'd go to Tennessee where no one knew me and I would start over. Carol would keep Michelle and Stan and little Jennifer.

None of this came out of rational thinking. I simply wanted to run away from everybody. Probably I wanted most of all to run away from myself.

In a crazy kind of way I planned out exactly what I would do. I was driving our Chevy station wagon to our house on the north side of Atlanta. I knew each thing I would do. First, I would pull up at the house and walk calmly inside. "Carol," I planned to say, "I'm leaving and I don't know where I'm going or if I'll ever be back again. I don't need you, I'm leaving, and I don't want to talk about it."

I envisioned myself pushing past her, going into our bedroom and packing a few clothes, and then leaving the house and driving away. They could have the house and anything else of mine. I didn't care. I only wanted to be free from responsibility, from trying to make a living, from fighting to keep my head above the waters of bills and problems. My self-esteem, which I had struggled with most of my life, reached a new low.

Nothing's going to stop me this time! I thought. I felt a surge of energy, greater than I had known in weeks. *I'm leaving today!* (I was soon to be reminded that haughty statements like that always return to haunt you.)

I was driving on the east side of Interstate 285, which encircles Atlanta. Something distracted me for a minute, like the smell of burning rubber. Glancing hastily around I saw nothing alongside the road. I shrugged, no longer wondering what it was. I had more important things to think about.

The odor again. Strange that it should be getting stronger. At that time I reached my exit and pulled off. The odor increased. For the first time it occurred to me that it might be coming from under the hood of my car.

A few hundred feet from the expressway ramp I saw a shopping center. I pulled in to the parking lot, cut my engine, and jumped out of the car. Just as I jumped out, flames started shooting out from under the hood and I realized it was an electrical fire.

I could only think of running away. In the movies when a fire starts, the car always blows up, so I ran from it. It never exploded, although the car burst into flames; the vehicle was charred beyond recognition. Helplessly I watched the flames licking away. Someone must have called the fire department because I heard the sirens coming closer. But it was too late.

I stood there, hardly able to believe what had happened. Then I became enraged. *I couldn't even run away. I couldn't do anything right.*

I had only wanted to drive off to Tennessee or Arkansas, to start life over again. Now I couldn't do anything.

Finally I went to a telephone booth and dialed Carol. It appeared that I did need her after all.

"You've got to come and get me," I demanded. I told her where.

"What happened?"

"You'll never believe this, but our Chevy just burned up."

"What?"

"Just get over here." Still too angry to reason properly, I didn't care how mean I sounded.

In minutes Carol arrived and picked me up. I stayed sullen all the way home. She assumed I was upset over the loss of the car. I was more upset because it had wiped out my plan for freedom.

In the next few weeks, life changed for us. We began to communicate again—we had to. I had no job, no place to go, and no prospects. Carol taught school, so I had to coordinate using the car, getting her to work, picking her up, and making sure the kids got picked up from activities and programs.

The only bright spot was that I was beginning to open up and talk more to Carol. We continued going to church—five of us crammed into the VW bug. But I didn't talk about God or allow any of those fanatics from the First Baptist Church to talk to me either.

My depression grew.

"There's got to be something more to life than this," I said to myself a dozen times. "If there isn't something better, it just isn't worth living."

At my moment of great darkness I was on the verge of finding out how good life could be.

On Father's Day 1981 our family went to the First Baptist Church in Atlanta where Charles Stanley is pastor. I had been listening to him for weeks, but nothing particular had happened.

That day Dr. Stanley's sermon title was "Be Anxious in Nothing," and he took his text from Philippians 4:6. He began his sermon, "You've got financial problems, marital problems, problems at work, problems with your children. God says be anxious for nothing. No matter what your situation, don't be anxious."

As I listened I thought, "Dr. Stanley, you don't understand my situation or you wouldn't say those words."

I had hardly thought that when Dr. Stanley said, "You're probably sitting there saying, 'But you don't understand my situation.' "

I could hardly believe what I heard. For the next five or ten minutes, every time I raised a question in my mind, Dr. Stanley responded with an answer. I felt as though I were carrying on a dialogue with God, and Dr. Stanley was eavesdropping and then speaking back to me what God answered. I sat in an auditorium packed with people. Yet as Dr. Stanley continued to preach, I felt as though I had been singled out and that the message was aimed just at me. I knew I couldn't run any further. I could no longer hide from God.

That afternoon, I went out for a run, the pain inside hurting so badly that I had to force myself to put one foot in front of the other. But I stopped before I finished even one mile. I stood in the street for a long time, not caring if a car hit me—secretly hoping that I would be hit so that I wouldn't have to struggle anymore.

There was a wooded area nearby and without realizing what I was doing, I ran into the woods and fell to the ground. I was so miserable and I hurt so badly inside.

"Oh, God!" I moaned. Again and again I repeated those two words. "Oh, God!" As I've tried to explain this, I hardly know how to put into words the deep misery I felt. Everything I had done, every failure, and every mistake tormented me.

"God, I'm so despicable. I hate myself and I hate life. If there's anything You can salvage, You can have it. I'm weak and useless."

Then the tears flowed and I couldn't even say another word. I lay there crying for a long time and I made no effort to stop the tears.

Time was suspended and I lay there. Slowly the tears stopped, and as they did a peace came over me. Nothing exceptional happened, except, for the first time in weeks, I didn't hate myself and the world around me.

Finally I got up, wiped my tear-streaked face on my T-shirt and started running again. Those legs that before could hardly move received a sudden infusion of energy. I must have run for two or three hours. When I finally returned home, I felt at peace.

Other than the peace I felt inside, life had not changed. I still had no job and even though deals kept coming my way, for some strange reason, they kept falling apart.

About a week after my experience, people who knew us said things to Carol such as, "Stan's changed lately. Have you noticed?"

"He's more peaceful and calm."

"Stan's easier to talk to than he used to be."

I didn't see any significant change going on in my life, yet I knew I was different. Different in a way I couldn't explain or even try to, but I knew I had changed.

On reflection, I can easily call that my real conversion to Jesus Christ. But events happened so gradually after that initial experience that I hardly realized what was going on.

Ups and downs still came, but I had changed. More people noticed and many of them told me. I vaguely realized that I no longer stormed at Carol or yelled at the children. Even more astounding, as each of the projects fell through, I was able to say, "Guess that one wasn't right for me."

Eventually I could say even more confidently, "That's not what God wants for us." That change in expression reflected the way I had evolved. I slowly understood that God was in my life and would help me, if I'd let Him.

Approximately a month after Dr. Stanley's sermon. the money factor changed, too. Through Tyler I met Ara Kalpak, regional vice-president of the A. L. Williams Insurance Company. Ara then introduced me to Bo Adams and A. L. ("Art") Williams, who hired me for twenty-four months (through mid-1983) to do speaking and motivation seminars for them. They guaranteed the money, whether they needed my services or not.

They even had me do a recruitment film, "The Greatest Challenge in America." I laughed when that opportunity came. I had once tried so hard to have a film made about my life and now, when I wasn't seeking it, I finally appeared in one.

At last I had gotten my priorities straight. God first and my family right behind Him. Then I could put my business life next. I had a new outlook and my life started turning around.

In July 1981, I loaned my name to a 10k race (6.2 miles) and an auto dealer publicized it all over the metropolitan Atlanta area. The come-on for the race was the free use of a new Ford for six months. Anyone could win who filled out an entry form, with the single stipulation that the person had to be present.

After the race, Carol, the children, and I were getting ready to leave just as they held the drawing. "Let's go," I said.

"Let's wait a minute," Carol said. "I'd like to see who wins the car."

"All right," I said, at the same time thinking, *wouldn't it be great if we could have that car for six months?* It could sure solve a lot of problems for us.

"The first number is. . . ."

Nobody responded. The man waited a full minute. He chatted about Fords and then said, "Since no one claimed the winning number, we're going to draw another." Then he read a second number.

Again silence. Again he extolled the virtues of his product while he waited.

"Here's the third chance," he said, and I could see he was beginning to get nervous because he wanted someone to claim that car.

"The next number is 352!"

For some reason, I had remembered the number of our ticket and I pulled it out. Sure enough, I held ticket number 352.

I raised my hand, yelled, and the whole family went wild. We went forward and got the keys to that brand-new Ford. A friend drove our VW so that all of us could have the initial ride together.

"Stan, don't you see God's hand at work in this?" Carol asked.

"Yeah, maybe," I answered. I hadn't put it all together, but I was beginning to feel the things happening in my life were more than coincidences.

"I've been praying for a second car," she said, and I knew she had. "This is God answering me."

"I suppose so," I said, but I wondered: was God at work, answering prayer? I didn't know.

I still made mistakes. I still fell back at times. But I was on my way up the mountain. Now I could say, "I've still got a long way to go, but God's with me. There's no mountain too high that *we* can't climb together." I said those words. Most of the time I sincerely believed them. I had my moments of doubt, but at least I was running in the right direction.

19

Could All This Be Coincidence?

Every long-distance run is a unique experience. There's no way to take a run for granted, whether it's for three days or eighty days. The event that taught me the most was my European run. I often refer to that as my eighty days in the wilderness.

Because I am self-disciplined and systematic I had everything all set up for the European run. We had an itinerary planned so specifically that I knew exactly where I was to start and stop every single day. This had all been coordinated and cleared with each government. Everything was set for me to leave for Europe on Monday, September 13, 1982.

I felt especially good because I had a great sponsor lined up for this run. People often don't understand this matter of sponsorship, but expenses mount up in an extensive run such as the one across Europe. Not only were there the transportation costs there and back, but the correspondence, the phone bills and other expenses, plus the run itself. I had my own living expenses and those of my crew.

For the run in Europe, I would need several Europeans to help us with local directions and give us assistance with the media in their country. Emmett Walker of Georgia was to do most of the driving of my back-up car, and my friend, Dr. Hugo Greiner, a specialist in sports medicine, would double as my personal physician and official photographer. We ended up employing eight Europeans, not all at once, but for the whole trip through twelve countries.

When I did The Run for America, the expenses were greater than I had anticipated and I barely broke even. This time a single sponsor had verbally agreed to pay all expenses and I would even make a little profit from it.

At 5:00 P.M. on Thursday, September 9, four days before I was to leave for Scotland where the race would start, the phone rang. The caller identified himself as an executive with the sponsoring company.

"Great to hear from you," I said.

"You may not think it's so great after you hear what I have to tell you," he answered.

"Well, what is it?"

"Stan, I'm sorry, but the company has decided not to sponsor you."

We talked several more minutes and he gave me all the reasons why they had pulled out. But understanding the reasons didn't really help. I felt deflated and rejected. I told my close friends and those involved with me on the trip.

"Go ahead and cancel it, Stan," more than one person said.

I could do that. Or postpone it until I had another sponsor lined up. Dozens of thoughts went through my head. I knew only one thing: the most ruinous thing possible had happened. After months of careful preparation and negotiation with twelve different governments, I simply didn't have the money to pay the bills.

Everyone around me kept telling me to cancel, but I'm a fighter. When people start telling me to give up that's the very thing that urges me on. I thought of Mr. McRedd who told me I couldn't make it in college. I thought of people who said I couldn't run across Kentucky, and of others who laughed when they heard about my run across America. I had gritted my teeth and gone on. And that was what I wanted to do now.

The three people who planned to accompany me to Europe gathered in our living room with Carol and me. We talked for hours.

"Maybe the time's not right," Emmett said. "If we wait a few more months, it might work out."

"We can announce you're not making the run," Hugo said. "Those things happen all the time. Even the president changes or cancels summit meetings."

Hardly realizing what I was saying, and with a conviction I had never felt before, I stared at each of them. "I can't give up. And I don't think it's just my stubbornness."

"But look at the facts—"

"I feel strong about this, maybe stronger than anything else I've ever done before, because I know it's right," I said. I took a deep breath. "Let's wait until noon tomorrow. If God wants me to make that run, then we'll let God help. If nothing has happened by noon Friday, I'll call the whole thing off."

Although we talked a little more, everyone agreed. We would wait until noon the next day.

"With so many closed doors," I said, "maybe we need to try a different one."

The others thought I was making a valiant effort to hang on. I was, of course, and I didn't want to give up without a fight. But something within me—I now call it faith—made me know that I was to make that run across Europe.

"I just can't give up. Not yet." I must have said those words two dozen times during the evening.

Shortly after nine that night the phone rang. It had been ringing most of the evening with messages from well-wishers. I didn't have the heart to tell any of them of the latest development. Also, I felt that to admit the predicament to them meant the same as giving in.

This particular call came from Bruce Lorik who, along with my lawyer-friend Tyler, had been so instrumental in helping me turn to God. He, like the others, congratulated me and then we talked a little longer. "By the way, Stan," he said. "I talked today with Steve Brown, a man I've known a long time. He's a fine man and he's anxious to meet you."

I had heard of Steve Brown. He is president of the Fortune Group, which conducts sales management training all over the world. "Sure, I'd like to meet him sometime," I said, the words sounding empty because of my preoccupation.

Bruce went on: "He lives in Atlanta and he's home right now. I just finished talking to him. Why don't you give him a call?" He insisted on giving me Steve's number.

I didn't feel like talking to anyone, especially a complete stranger. I was in the midst of a personal crisis, but Bruce kept pressing. Finally I said, "Okay, Bruce, as soon as I hang up, I'll call."

A warm voice answered the phone and I introduced myself. "I'd like to meet you in person," Steve said.

"I'd like to meet you, too," I responded, stimulated by his enthusiasm.

"I know you do motivational speeches, too," he said. "Say, why don't you come into the office in the morning and let's have a chat."

"I guess I could do that," I said, trying to put an enthusiastic touch to my voice. Had it been another time, I would have been genuinely glad to meet and talk to Steve. From our conversation I felt that he might be interested in my working with him in the future, perhaps even doing motivational seminars with the Fortune Group. He didn't say that in our conversation but his voice hinted that this might be a possibility.

As soon as I hung up, I wondered if I ought to call back and cancel. I needed to go out and knock on corporate doors or make phone calls to find a new sponsor. Yet, going to see Steve Brown at least gave me something to do and I had no idea who else to contact for sponsorship.

Back in the living room, our group talked until midnight. Then, tired and unable to think of anything to do, we broke up. I had no sense of knowing how the problem would work out. I knew only one thing: I couldn't give up.

After they all left and I got into bed, however, doubts began to form in my mind. *Why you're plumb crazy, Stanley Cottrell,* I said to myself. *Who's going to come in at the last minute and sponsor some idiot to run across Europe?* I tried to purge the thought from my mind and knew I couldn't dwell on that. I had to hold on at least until Friday noon.

Beside my bed, I keep a notebook of clippings. When I read something that strikes me I keep it in that book. Sometimes when I can't sleep, I pick up the book and read one or two of the items. That night, unable to rest my mind, I let the notebook fall open at random and an article caught my eye, one that I hadn't remembered clipping. It was a newspaper column entitled "Never Give Up" by Dr. Charles Hagood, formerly the president of LaGrange College in Georgia. It said, in part:

> Remember how a victorious military group was described not as being braver than its defeated adversary, but as being brave five minutes longer.
>
> In those moments of weary despair when life is falling apart, we discover the stuff of which we're really made by our ability to go on. That strength we did not know we possessed is the bit of God's divine spirit planted in every human personality. None of us has a superior supply, but the difference comes in our willingness to hold on until His power is released.
>
> If you are just now hovering near the brink of collapse, take heart.

I could hardly believe what I had read. Every sentence hit as though written just for me. I felt as if God had spoken to me through that clipping.

I went to sleep that night, assured that somehow God would provide the financial backing for the European run.

The next morning, Steve and I met and had a pleasant time together. Several members of his board came in and we also talked and got acquainted. Such a congenial group. They kept asking me about myself and my running. The subject of the European run came up. I explained how it worked.

Then I added, "I may have to cancel it because last night my sponsor, faced with internal problems and a cash-flow crunch, backed out."

They sympathized with me and kept asking questions about how long I ran each day, how many days I would run in Europe, how I kept going—the usual questions people throw at me. I felt they genuinely wanted to know, so I answered.

I kept talking while a part of me whispered, "Stan, you need to get out of here. You've got to hunt for a sponsor."

I looked at the clock: 11:53. I groaned inwardly, only seven minutes to the deadline and I still couldn't figure out a way to raise the money. I tried to relax, thinking that I could run a month late; by then I could set up a different sponsor.

"Stan, do you realize the absurdity of your situation?" Steve asked. "Here it's almost noon on Friday and you're scheduled to leave on Monday and you don't have the money."

"Yessir," I said, "I very well know the situation. It takes a man of rare courage and vision to seize upon such an opportunity as this run." Immediately upon saying that, I thought: *Stan, you've blown it this time.*

He nodded his head in approval and said, "You know, I feel good about what you're trying to do. We need more people with a world vision. It could be such a fun thing, too."

Steve paused, glanced at the others in the group, and then back at me. "Stan, you've got your money. The Fortune Group will sponsor you."

I could hardly believe what I heard. Just at that moment I glanced at the time. It was 11:55. We had beaten the deadline by five minutes. Had God answered our prayers? I recalled the time Carol thought He had answered prayer when we won the car at the 10k race. I wasn't sure what had happened then and I wasn't quite sure what had happened now. But one thing I was sure of, the coincidences seemed to really be piling up.

20
Touring Europe the Hard Way

Had I needed any assurance about making the European trip, I didn't need it now. I was on my way. We left Atlanta on September 15 and went immediately to Cologne, Germany, where for two days doctors and medical researchers at the Institute for Circulation Research put me through every kind of medical examination appropriate to my running. I felt like a laboratory guinea pig.

On Sunday, September 19, we arrived in Edinburgh, Scotland, where the run was to officially begin. I met local people the day I arrived and their warmth and kindness impressed me as much as the beautiful scenery.

Ruth Graham, the wife of Evangelist Billy Graham, had arranged for me to meet Mrs. Jenny Summerville, sister of Eric Liddell, the Olympic medalist of "Chariots of Fire" fame. Mrs. Summerville is elderly and charming. At first she was a little suspicious of our motives, and I can understand that because of all the publicity that accompanied the release of the film, "Chariots of Fire." She had had many visitors, some who had made unreasonable demands of her. Yet, she welcomed us graciously and, once we got to know each other, she opened herself and her home to us.

Advance publicity brought reporters from the British Broadcasting Company and major British newspapers to her door for the scheduled beginning of the run the following day, September 20. It would have been a great send-off except for one thing. Only minutes before I was to start running, a heavy rain struck Edinburgh and showed no signs of quitting.

One of the reporters said, half joking, "They say that the sun always shines on the righteous, but this is ridiculous. Do you have any comments about that?"

I didn't know what to say. At the time I didn't yet know that the Scripture actually says, "He makes the rain to fall on the just and on the unjust." The persistent thunder and lightning might have deterred me from beginning on time, yet I knew God had worked out everything for me to run across Europe. I determined right then that nothing would stop me.

I took off, feeling the rain striking me like cold needles piercing my skin. I had run in rain before, but I had never run in so much rain. For the next twenty-two days, it rained almost every day. I kept wondering if it would ever stop.

The persistent rain took its toll on me physically. For instance, on the fourth day I developed shin splints in my left leg. In all my years of running this had never happened before although it's a common ailment to runners. I'm sure it came about because of the hilly terrain of Scotland and England. My left knee felt as if I had a nail embedded in it. Every time my left foot hit the pavement, a fresh stab of pain shot through me. It increased as I kept running.

I kept praying for God's help as I ran, and I refused to slow down. Surprisingly, after three more days the terrain leveled and the pain eased. At the end of Day 6, September 25, I wrote in my log book:

> I ran like a "bunny" today. I breezed thru 36 miles with virtually no discomfort. Hugo said I was looking like an athletic dude!

The following day was different:

> 1:00. Taking a fruit break. The wind is coming head on at 30-40 mph. I am really taking a beating. Running is out of the question. Walking is the only thing I can do today. My goal is to reach Dorchester which is only 19 miles away.

After running through Sherwood Forest, and Bed and Breakfast in a home where the English hospitality truly impressed us, I faced another difficult day.

> Wind once again greets me but with a force that almost knocks me off my feet. Already I know I have my days work cut out for me. I put into action all the tactics I have learned. Even Flow of Energy Distribution (EFED). Walk the hills, slow the pace down going into the winds.

On the thirteenth day we arrived in London from where we took a train to the coast and boarded a ferry for Rotterdam. On Day 17, October 6, I resumed the run from the Olympic Stadium in Amsterdam—my two new Dutch friends, Andrew and André, guiding the way past gorgeous waterways in Holland. Ten countries to go! And still, the rain persisted.

On the twentieth day, I ran along and for the first time doubted that I could complete the projected trip. My body, bruised and battered by the elements, especially from the driving rains, rebelled, telling me to quit. *What am I doing here anyway?* I asked myself. *A person has to be crazy to take punishment like this.* Even though I argued with myself, I kept putting one foot in front of the other. Yet it became obvious that I couldn't hold up much longer under this kind of weather. By noon running was out of the question because of the driving winds. I did the only thing I could: I walked.

On day 22, running from Brussels toward Luxembourg, dampness and cold penetrated my skin and every bone ached as if I had had an acute attack of arthritis. I hadn't felt warm since the run had begun. Physically, it had become the most painful run I'd ever made; I prayed constantly and still nothing seemed to happen. And then, about midday I got a break. I wrote in my log book that night:

> I start screaming My God, help me please—I just kept screaming. I couldn't stop. I turned my head to the right and couldn't believe it. There was a stone bldg. about the size of a smokehouse. There was a tablet stone over the open doorway—1849—and on top was a cross. It was like God saying, I know

you're here—I have not left you even in this storm, I hear you—
I love you.

Just a minute before I was crying God, just put your arms around me for a second. In that instant I gained strength—and the cold was gone . . . and to add to all this . . . 2 km. away I ran from under this black cloud into clear weather.

Suddenly I felt wonderful, knowing without a doubt that I would make it.

Two days later I learned something more about God's protective care. Even Hugo, who is not a particularly religious man, said, "God does all things good!" We entered the small Belgian town of L'eglise (which means "the church") and were shocked to see it in ruins. We were told that the first tornado in Belgian history had struck the town. No one was killed, but only the little chapel—about the size of our living room—was left standing. Our original schedule would have brought us through L'eglise on the day the tornado struck, but we were delayed in Amsterdam obtaining drivers. Realizing this, after we had taken pictures, I entered the chapel, sat down and prayed a prayer of thanksgiving to God for working things so perfectly in our lives.

I would have reason to be especially thankful on two other occasions on this journey. One came on Day 36, Monday, October 25. We had passed through Luxembourg, the eastern part of France, through the Black Forest and into Switzerland. I was running through mountains 1,000 meters high and the air was very cold. But my main concern was laundry.

So far as we could see, Europe knew nothing about laundromats! And no matter how we tried to disguise the smell of wet, sweat-soaked clothing, it was impossible. My drivers put my shoes under the seat of the station wagon, in a plastic bag, and my running clothes into a laundry bag, but it didn't matter. The whole car reeked. To make it worse, we passed through farm country and more than once behind open cattle trucks. On Day 36 I wrote:

Hugo is cussing like a sailor about the laundry. . . . He says if you want to stink—stink! As I run, I ask God, "Lord, I know you're

> plenty busy, but can you help me with something as insignificant as this little problem . . . ?" I almost felt ashamed of myself for even taking God's time to call on Him over this.

In a while I began the descent toward Lake Constance. The warmer air allowed me to shed my outer clothing. That night we checked in at a quaint and nice Gasthaus. After we had checked in, the owner's wife walked out to the car with us and saw the pile of obviously dirty clothes. She probably smelled them as well. In her thick accent she said, "You have many dirty clothes back there."

"Yes, ma'am, we sure do," I answered.

"I have a washing machine and dryer," she said. "I will take them tonight. When you leave in the morning they will be ready for you."

I was so exhilarated by her offer I grabbed her and kissed her on the forehead. I tried to explain to her what a wonderful answer to prayer she had been to us.

The next morning, we saw not only the washed clothes, but all of them ironed and neatly folded.

Two days later, during supper at a place where we stayed, an elderly man engaged Hugo in conversation.

"You are so very lucky," he said.

"Lucky? How do you mean?"

The man went on to say that this was the first time in 103 years that the mountain pass through which we had just come was not closed on this day. "In the memory of everyone around here, no one can tell of a year when the pass was not snowbound on this date," he said.

"Normally there's three feet of snow here," he said. "Everybody has been spending all day making preparations for themselves. It will be a long time before we can go across the pass again."

That night I went to bed, filled with thanksgiving in my heart. On Day 39, October 28, I recorded:

> We just hear . . . where I started running yesterday morning got a big snow yesterday and is snowed in today. God continues to protect and care and provide every need.

All during the run, Hugo was in touch with the sports academy in Cologne, where I would go immediately upon completing the run, for their further tests and examinations. On Day 42 I noted in my log book:

> 7:00—Hugo takes blood for the second time . . . from the arm and ear. He has all the equipment with him. He repeats the procedure tonight after we finish.

That day I started in Tutzing, running toward Garmisch-Partenkirchen in West Germany, where the Alps begin. Hugo took blood and urine tests and sent samples to Cologne by express train. I ran fifty kilometers* in six and a half hours—all for the purpose of the tests.

My route took me from Austria across northern Italy and along the French Mediterranean. Long after we had left the rains we continued to get into heavy winds. I had not foreseen this and didn't realize how hard it would be to run with high velocity winds working against me. On November 17, running east from Monaco, I had my personal worst speed—sixty-five minutes to go two miles. We found out later that the winds were 100 km. per hour (62 mph) that day. Again I prayed, "Lord, I can't keep going. I simply can't make it one more day."

While running in the mountains, where the road twists and turns, I had found that the wind was in my face one hour, and at my back the next hour. But on this particular day I was on a straight road. Yet, within an hour after I prayed the wind shifted. I couldn't figure out why, but I never argued about it. Suddenly, a tail wind seemed to push me on and I felt as if I were floating.

Saturday, November 20, brought me almost to the Spanish border. Our plan called for me to do forty kilometers by noon, but at 11 A.M. I had only done twenty-two. Then the wind changed. Instead of doing the sixty-five kilometers projected for the entire day, I didn't stop until I had completed eighty-three. My log read:

* A kilometer equals 3,280.8 ft., approximately 5/8 of a mile.

> Today I was in a trance running—just put my eyes about 15 feet in front of me and moved. I try to remember scriptures as much as I can. I miss going to church so very badly. I want to read and read the Bible. I really realize probably for the first time in my life where the real source of strength is and how God can take charge of everything if we will just get out of the way.

We stayed in Narrobone, France, that night and the evening meal was enormous and delectable. I wrote in the log book:

> I had a delicious pizza, pancakes, a fruit salad and whipped cream that was out of this world.

I didn't mind the ribbing Hugo and the others gave me for my capacity to put away the pasta and desserts. (Thanksgiving Day we made an exception, though not intentionally. We had fried eggs, pork and beans, and french fries.) My body was now in a seriously weakened condition. I had lost fourteen pounds. All my toenails were gone. My muscle glycogen and my body fat were dangerously low. Could a person in my condition go on?

Physical exhaustion began to work on me until I faced a crisis about the time we neared Barcelona. We had some 600 miles to go to our scheduled finish line, the Rock of Gibraltar. This meant another two weeks of running. I figured that I had already run 3,000 miles and that seemed more than enough. I was tempted to quit.

"Hugo," I groaned, "I'm worn out. I want to go home. Why don't we call a press conference at Barcelona and stop the run there?"

At first Hugo said nothing.

Again I told him that my body had been battered to pieces. "Three thousand miles is a lot of miles. We'll call a press conference at Barcelona and. . . . "

"Go ahead and quit. . . . "

"I have to," I said.

"*And,*" he interrupted me, "you go ahead and quit. No one told you to come out here. Quit! You are the only one who will suffer the embarrassment. Not me. Not any of the crew. All the world will remember you as someone who started out but quit just before reaching the goal."

Hugo wisely had said exactly the right thing. That spirit of determination rose up within me. "I can't quit!" I yelled.

Hugo grinned and said nothing more.

As my steps picked up their pace, I thought again of all the times in my life when I had felt inadequate. No matter how much I had accomplished in life up to this point, if I quit now, this is what others would remember. Maybe people wouldn't actually have felt that way, but in my mind, that's how I perceived them as feeling. *I'm going to finish this run,* I said to myself.

The rest of the day, when physical pains and unidentified throbbings surged through my body, I kept saying *I'm going to finish this run. There's no mountain too high that God and I can't climb together, and I'm going to do it.*

Later that day when exhaustion hit me so badly I didn't think I could go one mile farther, I prayed aloud, "God, I'll put my feet down if You keep picking them up. That's the only way I can complete this run." And as strange as it may sound to recount it, that's how I completed my run. Each time I put one foot down I envisioned God's hand lifting the other and letting go. One after the other.

On the evening of December 2, seventy-five days after leaving Jenny Summerville's home in Edinburgh, I saw my first sunset over the Atlantic Ocean. The water was a beautiful blue, the sun large and yellow. Stretched over the water was a gorgeous golden path that seemed to lead right to my feet. I imagined that "sun road" leading all the way across the ocean and to the doorstep of my home in Georgia, where lay my real gold, my family. I had talked with Carol and the children on many a night during my run across Europe. How their voices encouraged me and kept me going! Now, nearing the end of the run, I got a fresh boost of energy just knowing that within a week or so, I would be there with them.

On December 7, at 8:20 A.M., I saw the cold, impersonal Rock of

Gibraltar. As do most runners when they finally see the finish line ahead, I kicked my legs high and raced on. Two hundred feet from the border separating Spanish land from the British crown colony of Gibraltar I was stopped by border guards.

"You may not cross," they told me.

Many Spaniards congratulated me for finishing the run. From across the border, people waved and shouted congratulations. In the distance loomed the magnificent 1,396-foot Rock. I would not be able to get to it, but I was happy to realize I had completed the run. Happy and ecstatic. And I had finished on December 7, Momma's birthday.

Members of the European press asked me questions and took pictures, but I can hardly recall what I said to them. Hugo paid me the highest compliment: "Stanny boy," he said, "you are truly a super athletic dude!"

All I could think of was that I had completed the 3,500 miles, running from Edinburgh to Gibraltar in eighty days. And soon I was going home.

21
What Makes Stanley Run?

People often ask, "Why do you do those long runs?" I could give a cutesy answer such as "Because it's there." But I have three serious reasons why I run.

First, I run because I love it. Every long run sets up a new challenge. Whether we work in an office or take care of the home, we all need challenges in life. We especially need challenges in the areas we already have an interest in and some level of achievement. These experiences force us to grow. Once I found out that I could run, I kept doing it and kept pushing the limits. I have no idea how far or how long I can actually run. That's why I keep at this sport.

My whole life has centered around running. I'm forty years old. Many folks think that's the time for athletes to hang up their shoes. That's not how I see it. I'm just now getting into the best years of my running. At 35 I ran across Georgia. At 36, I set the record for the twenty-four-hour run. At 37 I ran across America. And at 39 I covered 3,500 miles in Europe. In between I also completed runs from Savannah to Atlanta (276 miles), from Nashville to Chattanooga (142 miles), and from Atlanta to Mobile, Alabama (386 miles) to benefit health organizations. I love the challenge of running and because I love it, I keep meeting new challenges.

Second, I run because I learn about myself. Every day I get up and race toward the goals I have set for myself. Like others, I need to press toward objectives just beyond my reach, the kind that demand effort and commitment. As I accept the challenge it makes me ask myself: *Why do I want to do this? What's so important about running?* I scrutinize my motives and monitor my attitudes. All of this results in a deeper level of self-understanding.

Third, long-distance running enables me to be more self-disciplined. The Apostle Paul wrote about keeping his body under control. Successful athletes do this as they learn to be in tune with themselves. Through my running, I'm so in tune with my body that I can tell when I've gained half a pound.

I'm striving to be the best I can be and to live my life to the fullest. Basically, I've always been a self-starter. I remember when, as a boy, I'd want to complain about getting up before daybreak on wintry mornings to milk the cows. Daddy never allowed me to argue. He would say: "It's a bitter pill, but it's got to be taken." In his own way he meant that it may be uncomfortable or inconvenient, but you have to do it.

I always got myself up and did my chores. In later years, with no one to push me, I had already learned to do what had to be done. Some mornings I would rather roll over and go back to sleep. But I won't let myself. Things need to be done and only I can do them.

Coming from a poor family I learned that you have to do some things simply because they have to get done. That has helped me later in life. I try to live by the philosophy, "Live every day as though it's your last, because one day it will be your last."

I want to live so that I get the maximum out of each day's activities and opportunities. I learned very early in life that you have to take whatever comes that day.

Since 1978 my physical achievements and endurance have attracted the attention of doctors who specialize in sports medicine. They have learned that we have different levels of physical achievement and physical fitness. This means that it's not fair to compare one sport with another or to compare my style of running with that of another runner. Some people run marathons (26.2 miles) very well. A few of them could run a marathon two days in a row and be all right. But most of them, if challenged to do the same thing for thirty

STAN'S VITAL STATISTICS

Birthdate	May 7, 1943
Average body weight	137 pounds
Normal blood pressure	90/70
Rested pulse rate	40
Hemoglobin count	15
Hematocrit	49.2
O^2 Uptake	70%

The Run Across Europe

	Before	After
Weight	138 pounds	131 pounds
Percent body fat	5.5%	3.5%
Average time per mile	7 min. 15 seconds	

days or fifty days straight, would fall apart. They don't train for that style of running and aren't equipped for it. Further, most of them wouldn't consider running those distances. I have a level of endurance that I have developed from childhood and it's different from the endurance level of other types of runners.

Recently someone pointed out to me that the kind of running I do is the equivalent of running two marathons *every day.* When I ran across Europe in 1982, for eighty days I averaged approximately two marathons a day. I could not do this if my body were not extremely fuel efficient.

For instance, the average runner burns between ninety and one hundred calories each mile. That means if a man ran sixty miles in one day he would need six thousand calories just for the run *plus* another two to three thousand calories to maintain body weight. On a sixty-mile run, that figures out to about twenty-five pounds of food and liquid. The average person would find it impossible to ingest that much food while running.

As the result of all kinds of testing—electroencephalograms, pulmonary function testing, echocardiography, treadmill stress studies—doctors have concluded that I burn only thirty-five to forty calories per mile, making me one of the most fuel-efficient humans that they have studied. They have compared me to the camel in the desert which can take great quantities of nourishment, store it, and go for long periods of time without additional nourishment. They've concluded that this is partly due to heredity and partly acquired ability.

An area of study, pioneered in Cologne, Germany, involves lactate levels. The body makes energy in two ways: (1) by using oxygen which we call aerobic production, and (2) without oxygen or anaerobic. When we exercise we need enough oxygen to produce the required amount of energy. If we get enough oxygen, we have no side effects. However, if we exercise and don't get enough oxygen (become anaerobic), our bodies produce chemicals, the main one being lactate. If we continue to exercise without sufficient oxygen, lactate builds and at high levels can cause harmful effects. At a certain level we reach the anaerobic threshold. We can even pass out. Some athletes build up such a lactate level in running a marathon that they require as long as six weeks to recuperate.

On the other hand, sports doctors have checked my lactate level after I have run all day, sometimes as far as sixty miles, and found that my lactate reached only 1.9. (Anaerobic is 4.0.)

Studies in body fat capture a lot of attention today. Obviously, the more body fat a person has, the lower will be his performance level. Carrying extra weight, like having weights strapped to the back, hinders top performance. Nutritionists estimate that the average man in the United States has about sixteen percent body fat, and the average woman nineteen percent. Tests indicate that I have about three to four percent body fat. Well-toned athletes have about nine or ten percent body fat.

On a run, my nutritional needs are crucially important. I make sure that my diet consists of at least 70 percent complex carbohydrates. Fats found in cheese help keep my percent body fat from getting dangerously low. My feeling is that most athletes should maintain a level of at least five percent.

I am often asked about my training. I don't do the "typical" calisthenics but rather, I do light stretching and very light weight work with high repetitions. Most of all, I do the thing that I like doing all the time; I run. I average between 100 and 150 miles a week. By running at that level I am usually ready to take on any kind of run.

As far as training for actual running events, I started out as most runners do in this country, using the interval method. I'm now convinced that this is not only a poor method; I think it's absolutely harmful.

Developed in Germany in the 1930s and modified by American coaches, interval training consists of repeated hard runs over a measured distance, followed by recovery periods (intervals) of relaxed jogging.

For example, most interval running suggests that people should hit top speed for a particular distance, then slow to a jog, and then return to a fast pace. Typically, the coach makes a man run 440 yards twenty times, each time under seventy seconds. Between each 440-yard dash, he slowly jogs 220 yards for recovery. That means he gets less than a minute of recovery between each 440. This puts the body under heavy stress and into a truly pathological state. Coaches knew this happened, but theorized that a man could get used to it, build himself up and not become fatigued. The latest research points out what I've always believed, that the body cannot get used to it.

When the body is put under such stress, it can't get enough oxygen. Therefore, it can't rid itself of carbon dioxide, the waste product of metabolism. When this happens, the body produces lactic acid (or as I prefer to call it, fatigue poisoning). If it continues, the body actually breaks down through exhaustion. A runner can even pass out.

Interval training was popular because it was thought to be the method that would bring an athlete to his or her peak level of fitness in the shortest period of time. But I am convinced that it is harmful and that numerous potential Olympic athletes have been ruined by using this method.

I was 32 before I discovered the harmful effects of interval running. In the 1970s I began to hear of Long Slow Distance (LSD). It appealed to me as an alternative because it is the more natural way to train.

Basically, LSD says that a person should run longer distances at slower speeds. By this method, the runner develops greater cardiovascular integrity, meaning greater strength. His maximum speed is a result of his greater strength.

Experts who advocate LSD say that when two people can carry on a conversation and still run, they are traveling at the correct rate of speed. I can carry on a conversation while running a mile in seven minutes, a little faster than most people. I've run that way since I was a child.

When I am training I put away the stop watch and run at a conversational pace. If I can talk and still run without getting out of breath I'm running at a good rate of speed for me. Running like this prevents a buildup of lactate acid.

The only kind of special training I ever do is tempo running. Once a week I run at my usual, conversational pace and then gradually increase the pace for a short time, followed by a gradual decrease in the pace. Over a two-hour period I might speed up like this as many as ten times.

When I do long cross-country runs, people sometimes ask about my recovery. I learned the hard way to let the body wind down.

After completing the European run, I stopped running for several days. A sudden and deep depression came over me and I constantly had to fight against it. Then it dawned on me that I experienced a natural result of non-running.

The body manufactures what we call endorphines, a morphine-like chemical that is a natural stimulant. For eighty days my body had released these chemicals and, much like morphine, I became addicted to them. Then, suddenly cutting off my supply by not running produced an adverse effect much like withdrawal symptoms from drug addiction, although less severe.

I know now that the way to recover from a long run is to cut down the mileage gradually. If, for example, I ran fifty miles a day for an extended period, and then completed the run, I could not just quit running and rest. Rather, I learned to reduce my mileage to forty miles the day after the completion of the long-distance run, and then to thirty, until I reached my normal twenty miles a day. By gradually reducing my running, I can recover without any physical or psychological difficulty.

Most runners cannot continuously subject their bodies to the kind of pounding required of an ultramarathoner. Sports doctors now advise marathon runners not to exceed three such runs—26.2 miles—a year. They tell them that in running a marathon they actually destroy about six percent of the muscle tissue which takes approximately six weeks to rebuild. The experts tell a runner to rest and not run at all for three days after a marathon.

Obviously, I don't follow the rules for a typical marathoner. Through some quirk of nature (or by God's design, whichever you care to say), my body functions differently.

While you need a special body to be an ultramarathoner, you also need something going on inside your head. Sometimes when I'm a little unsure of myself I remember something Momma still says to me, "Son, there's nothing you can't do with the good Lord's help."

That's a great lesson I've learned: I need God, every day. I've even learned a verse from the Bible which I quote to myself regularly: "I can do all things through Christ who strengthens me."

I have also learned that I need people. I can't make it in life alone. I need the support, encouragement, and friendship of others.

As far back as the late 1970s I wanted my running to be more than a sporting event. When the Kentucky Lung Association sponsored my run across Kentucky in 1979, I saw for the first time that my idea had possibilities. I could promote fitness, preventative medicine, and still run.

When I ran across America, people along the way greeted me, shook hands and cheered me on. Almost every day a few of them ran part of the way with me. Sometimes they slipped a piece of paper into my hand with their name and address on it. I tried to follow up these people and have remained in contact with many of them.

I've always been a "people person" anyway. But interacting with people has become especially important to me since my religious conversion. Since then I've prayed that God will help me live every day of my life in such a way that every person with whom I come in contact. will be positively influenced. I want to promote trust and understanding among people, regardless of their race or culture.

"Wouldn't it be wonderful," I asked a friend one day, "if God would use me to promote friendship and understanding among peoples and nations, just through my running?"

"Why not?" he answered. "Sounds like a good idea."

And why not? I shrugged off the idea then, but it kept coming back.

On my run across Europe I experienced the same friendliness among people whom I had never met. Some of them, I learned, had waited for hours to see me run past. That really touched me. Often, I would stop and greet them. I would hug them and they would reciprocate warmly.

While running across Europe this desire of mine came into sharp focus. It was as though the shutter of a camera opened for a split second and I saw a sea of faces—people of varied backgrounds, all being friends with one another. That is when my biggest dream was born—Friendship Sports. I visualized whole nations being brought together as people from each country reach out to one another.

In January 1983, a month after I had returned to the United States following that run, I had an appointment with a successful Atlanta businessman, Sonny Bonner. Sonny lives by his religious convictions and it shows. He has taught me a lot by the way he cares about people.

During our conversation he prayed for me and for my success in promoting friendship through my runs. Then he said, "Stan, I'd like to give you a little advice."

"Of course. Just tell me."

"Incorporate yourself into a nonprofit organization," he said. Being aware of the constant problem of getting sponsors for my runs, he suggested that if I were sponsored by a nonprofit organization, people could make tax-free contributions. "People who believe in what you're doing can stand behind you financially."

I had some reservations about the idea. We continued to talk.

Then Sonny said something that really made sense. "Look at it this way," he said. "This is your ministry. You bring a unique talent to the world. Think of the opportunities you have. You can contact people no one else can. You can talk to them about friendship, fitness, even about God. You can pass out Bibles and pamphlets if you want. Speak at seminars. Hold workshops."

Immediately a new idea was born. Stadium-to-stadium runs. I thought to myself. Instead of merely running from one city to another, why not run from the stadium of one city to that of another? Prior to my arrival in the second city, local organizations could be enlisted there to cooperate and fill the stadium with teenagers. I saw this all as clearly as if it had already happened. I would complete a forty-mile run by dashing into a sports arena filled with teens. I would speak, challenging them to live by the highest ideals, to strive to be champions. Then I would prepare to go on to the next city. I envisioned running 300 to 500 miles, stopping at four or five cities along the way over a period of a few days. We would bypass larger metropolitan areas, but stop in the smaller cities, where the total population would be less than 200,000. I saw myself talking to children and young people in schools. I have already done this wherever I've run and on many occasions the schools dismissed classes so that the children could stand alongside the road and wave me on. I've stopped and spoken to those children for five minutes, trying to motivate them toward doing their very best for themselves and their school.

In the spring of 1983 I took Sonny's advice and incorporated my running efforts and interests under the name: Friendship Sports Association, Incorporated.

In May 1983 I did my first true friendship run, in the Dominican Republic. The year before, I had visited the island and at a press conference called by the minister of tourism I promised to return after my run across Europe.

The members of the press in Santo Domingo seemed all prepared to build me up as some sort of superman. They could not get over the fact that I had run across America and that I was soon to run through twelve countries of Europe. The old Stan Cottrell thrived on the sort of attention they were giving me, but as the questions continued to center more and more on my achievements, I began thinking: *Lord, how can I tell them that I'm really running for You now?*

Just then a reporter asked, "Are you a religious man?"

"When you see Stan Cottrell run," I told him, "you can just imagine Christ Jesus going ahead of me every step of the way."

In December 1982 I began putting the final touches on plans to run across the Dominican Republic. I've learned that these things require a lot of advance planning and everything from food and clothing to the weather conditions must be considered. The tropical heat in the Dominican Republic was one element that I had not encountered before. This is where Hugo Greiner proved of invaluable assistance. He saw to it that I had adequate liquids for the run, and plenty of sunscreen protection for my skin. The run—dubbed the Dominican Republic Tropical Paradise Friendship Run—was held in May 1983.

When I first arrived I encountered a wall of formality. Some nationals, quite rightly, were suspicious of me, thinking I had some exploitative purpose in mind. No one treated me rude but they remained reserved even while giving me quite a bit of press and TV coverage as I started out at Porta Plata, running to Santo Domingo.

The turning point came because the minister of tourism, Dr. Rafael Subervi Bonilla, sent two of his aides to accompany the back-up crew on the road. They saw us as real human beings who had not come to get involved in political issues, but who honestly wanted to spread friendship. By the end of the run the barriers of formality had collapsed. I felt that I had formed true friendships with many people of the Dominican Republic.

Nowhere was this more evident to me than at the banquet Dr. Subervi arranged for us at the conclusion of the run. It lasted three hours. I can't describe the feeling of camaraderie that prevailed. Dignitaries proposed one toast after another to America and spoke of their desire for ongoing friendship with people around the globe.

One official there didn't simply *ask* me to return for a second run. He insisted on it, adding, "You have laid a strong foundation for friendship in our land." I just breathed a prayer of thanks for that. My dream of building friendship among peoples was coming true. In March 1984 I returned for another Dominican run, and that led to the Friendship Mission Run through Jamaica in May 1984.

Since then I've continued to think of ways to promote friendship. After all, everyone needs friends. I don't know how much I can do as one individual, but I want to do whatever possible to break down barriers between nations, cultures, and races. I have no intention of jumping into political issues or spreading middle class western values. I run. That's what I do best. And I intend to use this ability to call people together and to promote harmony.

I still have a lot of unfulfilled dreams, but I don't intend to let them remain unfulfilled. For five years I've dreamed of running across the Great Wall of China. In 1981 everything almost fell into place for this run, but at the last minute the political winds blew cold. The run was cancelled.

But my dream wouldn't let go. With the help of individuals like Mrs. Ruth Bell Graham, who was born in China, and others too numerous to name, from all branches of our state and federal government, I was able to present my dream of a friendship run in Peking (Beijing) in December 1983. I returned home with this signed authorization from the China Sports Service Company:

> After two years of contacts, Mr. Stan Cottrell met, in Beijing on December 20, 1983, with Mr. Kong Qingwen of China Sports Service Company (C.S.S.) and discussed, with mutual trust and respect, the proposed event of the "Great Friendship Run."
>
> Both are in agreement that this event will not only be beneficial to the promotion of the friendship and mutual understanding between the peoples of China and the United States, but also helpful to the development of the sport of running. C.S.S., therefore, would like to have close cooperation with Mr. Cottrell and his organization to make this event a success.

> The "Great Friendship Run" will begin at the Great Wall in Beijing in October 1984 and conclude in the city of Guangzhou. . . .

With a full and thankful heart I returned from Peking to my family just before Christmas 1983. The long-dreamed-of Great Friendship Run is a step closer to reality. It is scheduled to begin on October 1 and to take approximately fifty-five days.

Other friendship runs on other continents are among my dreams as well. I hope, God willing, to be able to run through the main islands of Japan, in Australia, in South America, and across the southern tip of Africa. With God's help I will see these dreams fulfilled. It will be a long while before I hang up my running shoes for good. After all, dreams, hopes, and imagination are all real, aren't they?

That is the way I live, always having one more goal yet in front of me, always straining to reach that next challenge. I'm always climbing the next mountain.

Experience tells me that when I commit myself to a goal, hold on, and keep trying, I can do it—as long as I remember a most important qualifier. With God! There's no mountain too high anymore—not a single one—*with God.* I know that I can do all things through Christ who strengthens me.

I know that more than ever now because of one other run I haven't told you about. That run had to do with some unfinished business between Daddy and me.

22
Highest Mountain of Them All

When I could not run in China in 1981, I turned my attention to a mountain that twice had eluded me. I had run across Georgia. I had set the world record for running the most distance in twenty-four hours. I had run across America. But I had not been able to run across Kentucky. To my mind, this was what my father would call "unfinished business."

I had promised myself—and Daddy—that I would return one day and make it on foot from one end of Kentucky to the other. Early summer 1981 found me in top condition physically. Due to some long distance runs I had done earlier in the year, I decided it was time to take care of this unfinished business that had been gnawing on me.

In June I picked up the phone and called the Kentucky Lung Association. Barry Gottschalk, the public relations director, answered.

I told Barry: "I know I failed before and I know you all put a lot of time and effort and money into it, but do you think you could take a chance with me one more time? I'd like to come back this fall and run across Kentucky. And I'd be tickled if the Kentucky Lung Association would see fit to sponsor it."

Barry was interested. Before he got off the phone I added, "You can be sure that I'll be ready this time—even it it comes a blizzard."

Barry talked it over with the association's executive committee and in a few days he phoned to say, "All systems are go."

The date of October 24 was selected. The timing would be perfect, he said, to kick off the state Christmas Seal campaign.

From June through mid-October I trained on Georgia roads, taking time in August to take part in a local twenty-four-hour relay run. In Kentucky the word was getting out: Stan Cottrell is going to try again.

Barry arranged telephone interviews for me on some of the state's radio stations and a full-page advertisement appeared in the *Courier-Journal,* paid for by the Lung Association.

Before I left home for Kentucky, Carol expressed her concern. "Honey, I know why you want to do this," she said. "But this time I'm afraid you're going to hurt yourself bad."

She understood me perfectly. She knew that this time it was do or die. She feared that if I injured myself while on the road I wouldn't stop. And, of course, Daddy would not be there beside the road if anything happened. Assuring her that I would be sensible, I went to Kentucky.

In Munfordville the day before the run the townspeople were excited. Old-timers who knew me kidded: "You know, we're getting tired of this. Will you please come on and get this thing over with!" In their good-natured way they showed that they were behind me a hundred percent.

At Momma's place I met my brother Harold who had driven in from Lexington for the occasion. Before I got there, he had been down to the woods at the lower end of our property and he had a surprise for me.

"This is a special, special occasion," he said as he came up to me. Then he took from behind him the largest ginseng root I had ever seen.

"Daddy planted this about ten years ago down by the big oak tree," he added. "I want you to take some of this root along with you on the run. Remember how Daddy used to say it would do wonders for your running? You don't need much—just a little bitty piece between your cheek and gum."

We laughed. Daddy had always been big on ginseng. And he had tried, without success, to persuade me to chew on a little ginseng while I ran. I had since learned that many European athletes take powdered ginseng in capsule form. It is supposed to increase cardiovascular function. I was glad to accept Harold's gift and was touched by his support. The ginseng would be a special reminder of Daddy. And who knows? Maybe it would help.

I was to follow the same route across Kentucky that I had previously attempted. Beginning at the Kentucky-Tennessee line, just below Franklin, I would follow Highway 31 all the way to the Ohio River at Louisville. It would not be an easy run. Kentucky is a land of rolling hills—"knobs" we call them. The Muldraugh region just north of Fort Knox would present a particular challenge. Yet, everything in me said *go*. I was in topnotch condition and I was in touch with God. He would be my strength.

The run was scheduled to begin at four A.M. on Monday, October 24. It would be almost a nonstop effort and the plan called for me to arrive at the Belvedere, a modern office-hotel complex on the Ohio River in Louisville, at noon the next day. I had thirty-two hours to cover 146 miles.

Two vans and a couple of mopeds provided by the Lung Association would accompany me the length of the trip. State and local police would be along as escorts, especially through the cities. My own crew consisted of two top runners, Chuck Harris and Bob Crosby, whom I had brought with me from Georgia. They would drive a van carrying my extra clothing and supplies.

Joining the entourage for the start of the run were my good friends from Munfordville, Mayor Jim Berry and Bob Chambliss, a banker. With them was a young preacher and friend of the family, Mike Withrow. I was glad he was there and before the run got started I asked him to pray. Under a canopy of stars on that clear Kentucky morning, we bowed our heads while Mike asked the Lord to bless the trip, to give me strength and courage, and that somehow He would be glorified in it.

After handshakes I was on the road. The last thing I heard as I broke into a stride was Chuck calling to Bob: "Does he have the root? Did you give him the root?" With a light heart I set out on the road. Yes, I had "the root."

The temperature was about 38° that morning. The forecast called for clear conditions all the way. But just in case, I had come prepared. In the van were gloves, stocking cap, polypropylene underwear and Gore-tex outer clothing—the whole bit.

A handful of runners started out with me and ran ahead. But I paced myself, following all the rules I had set for myself. This was a serious thing with me—as serious as anything I had ever done.

Just as I reached Bowling Green the sun was coming up. A flood of memories filled my mind when I came to the bridge spanning the Green River there. Many a time I had stood just beyond the bridge and hitchhiked home from college to help Daddy on the weekend.

In town I stopped long enough to talk to some of the people standing by, waiting for me to pass. A member of the broadcast staff of a local radio station was there to greet me and report on my progress. "At this point, he's feeling fine," I heard him say into his mike.

As I headed toward Munfordville, Charlie Locke of the Lung Association commented: "Stan, buddy, you're running so smoothly. I can't believe how relaxed you look and how easy you're running."

I was running an almost perfect pace and feeling great. *Even flow of energy distribution* I kept telling myself. I imagined my body as one big fuel cell good for 146 miles, and I didn't want to burn that energy too soon. Feeling strong and confident and eager to complete the run, I had to make use of what my years of running had taught me and not burn out.

I ran according to my usual long distance plan—run fifteen minutes followed by five minutes of walking, run fifteen and walk five. Chuck and Bob were amazed that I seemed to know exactly when fifteen minutes were up. I would raise my hand to signal that it was time to slow down and walk just as their stopwatches showed fifteen minutes had elapsed. According to my plan, after each three hours I took a complete break for rest and nourishment.

Entering Park City I was greeted by a group of people who claimed to be my fourth cousins. They savored this moment with me and they served to boost my spirits even more. One or two in the group knew me from college and remembered that at college I was called "Wild Bull," a not too complimentary tag given me because of my bad temper. But now it was in jest that they called out, "Wild Bull's still at it!"

Maybe it was the extreme contrast in my emotions that made such an impression on me as I neared Cave City. All along the way I had felt higher than a Georgia pine, my spirits just soaring—till I reached Cave City. That was where, on my second attempt, Daddy had met me in the rain with his pickup.

As I approached the spot I could almost see Daddy's truck with that sign pasted on the side: "I'm a Fox Hunter and a Good Sport." The memories of that earlier run came back so vividly it was as though it were happening all over again. The tears flowed. I kept running, but my mind and emotions were still back there near Cave City where Daddy had told me to get into the pickup.

A fellow on a moped who paced me a few miles must have noticed that I was crying. "What's wrong?" he asked. I didn't even respond. How could I tell him that I had relived one of the most meaningful experiences in my life? In that moment I realized afresh that Daddy had been proud of me—not only for that attempted run, but all along, even though he didn't know how to say it.

"I won't let you down this time, Daddy," I whispered. He wouldn't be pulling up beside me. Daddy was dead, but I felt his presence very close to me. "I'll make it this time," I said, and chewed hard on the ginseng root. Its juices flowed—and so did the tears. It was an awesome experience to be running now, under a clear noon-day sky, so conscious of Daddy's presence.

When I reached Munfordville, it seemed that people came out of the woodwork. Tommy Joe Turner, who twenty years earlier had bet me that I couldn't run from Horse Cave to Munfordville, was there with the city fire truck, giving me a grand welcome.

And of course, there was Momma. I stopped only for a short break because I didn't want anything to interrupt my progress toward the ultimate goal. The Chamber of Commerce gave Momma a bouquet of roses and the newspaper took a picture of the two of us, arm in arm.

"Don't forget the good Lord," she said as I got ready to resume the run. "He'll pull you through."

Momma's faith in me buoyed my spirits once again, as did the presence of people who lined the highway. It seemed that a thousand people had turned out along the road through Munfordville. It was excellent publicity for the Lung Association.

By sundown I had traveled ninety-three miles. Only fifty more to go. The sky remained clear. Would the weather hold? I recalled the incredible storms that had blown up from out of nowhere on the second run in 1976.

"Don't let it happen tonight, Lord—please!" I prayed.

Before midnight we were in E-town, where I had run track and cross-country in high school. We were making such good time that we decided to check in at a motel and rest for three hours. I took a hot shower and had a rubdown. At three A.M. we were back on the road.

I had no trouble getting going again. Everything was going well—maybe too well. I kept wondering what would happen, what jinx would hit me in these last few miles and defeat me again.

At Fort Knox we waited for some runners who wanted to join me. I remember thinking, when we passed the gold vault at Fort Knox, *I'm going to make it. I know I'm going to make it!* I had only twenty-eight miles to go.

By 9:30 I reached the outskirts of Louisville, well ahead of schedule. Some fourteen miles remained, and I was feeling strong. Nothing could go wrong now. Television and radio people were coming out to meet me. I ran on effortlessly it seemed, following my police escorts.

Sirens blared and well-wishers waved to me. Once we reached downtown, I seemed to be flying along. At Broadway we turned and headed straight for the Belvedere and the Ohio River, and the finish line. Finally, Kentucky was conquered, and so were a lot of other things.

A few steps farther and I collapsed in the arms of Jerry Zimmerer, a board member of the Lung Association. My friends and many people I did not know surrounded me with congratulations. And amid the sea of faces I could almost see Daddy smiling at me, and saying, "Eee-ehh!"

I had kept my promise. I had climbed the highest mountain of them all and, truly, God was with me every step of the way.

STAN COTTRELL'S
Greenland
North
America
Europe
Dominican
Republic
Jamaica
South
America
N
W
E
S
1
2
3
4
5
6
7
8
9
14